Practical Resources for Teaching Citizenship in Secondary Classrooms

Ruth Tudor

David Fulton Publishers
London

David Fulton Publishers Ltd
The Chiswick Centre, 414 Chiswick High Road, London W4 5TF

www.fultonpublishers.co.uk

First published in Great Britain in 2002 by David Fulton Publishers

British Library Cataloguing in Publication Data
A catalogue record for this book is available from the British Library.

ISBN 1 85346 840 1

Typeset by Servis Filmsetting Ltd
Printed and bound in Great Britain by Bell and Bain Ltd, Glasgow

Practical Resources for Teaching Citizenship in Secondary Classrooms

Contents

Introduction

What is citizenship?

> We aim at no less than a change in the political culture of this country both nationally and locally: for people to think of themselves as active citizens, willing, able and equipped to have an influence in public life and with the critical capacities to weigh evidence before speaking and acting; to build on and to extend radically to young people the best in existing traditions of community involvement and public service, and to make them individually confident in finding new forms of involvement and acting among themselves.
>
> (Report on *Education for Citizenship and the Teaching of Democracy in Schools*, QCA 1998)

The passage above expresses the innovative and radical nature of citizenship education as it is intended to be realised within schools in England from August 2002. Citizenship education is not simply about knowing and understanding but is about knowing and understanding *through* doing and being. In citizenship education pupils participate, take action, reflect, think critically, negotiate. They learn to become informed and responsible citizens who are able to make a difference in their communities because their education has given them the knowledge, understanding and skills they need to do so, as well as positive experiences of real participation at school and within the local community.

The Citizenship Statutory Order

What does the Citizenship Statutory Order require schools to do at Key Stage 3?

Regarding teaching and learning
The Programmes of Study at Key Stage 3 (and 4) begin:

> Teachers should ensure that knowledge and understanding about becoming informed citizens are acquired and applied when developing skills of enquiry and communication, and participation and responsible action.
>
> (*Citizenship: The National Curriculum for England*, QCA 1999: 14)

Within this directive, the Citizenship Programme of Study is flexible. Schools can choose how to plan, approach and provide citizenship education. For example, the 'knowledge and understanding' aspects, including knowledge of rights, responsibilities, public services, law, government, British diversity, democracy can be delivered in different ways depending on the needs of the school. The main models adopted by schools are summarised below in the next main section. There are no requirements to study a particular theme in a particular order and the selection of topical examples and questions for each theme is up to individual schools or teachers.

Regarding assessment

At Key Stage 3 there is a statutory requirement for teacher assessment in citizenship education from August 2002. Teacher assessment is about assessing, recording and reporting on progress during the Key Stage as well as summarising achievement at the end of the Key Stage.

Teachers will make their end of key stage assessments in relation to a single Attainment Target for citizenship education, which consists of an end of key stage description. In subjects with end of key stage descriptions, teachers reach a judgement by using evidence of attainment and achievement over time, including written, practical and oral work. This judgement must be reported to parents/carers at end of the Key Stage. There is no requirement for schools to collect summary data of teacher assessments in citizenship education although evidence of achievement must be kept by schools.

The end of Key Stage 3 description of the attainment target in citizenship education states:

> Pupils have a broad knowledge and understanding of the topical events they study; the rights, responsibilities and duties of citizens; the role of the voluntary sector; forms of government; provision of public services; and the criminal and legal systems. They show how the public gets information and how opinion is formed and expressed, including through the media. They show understanding of how and why changes take place in society. Pupils take part in school and community-based activities, demonstrating personal and group responsibility in their attitudes to themselves and others.
>
> (From *Citizenship: The National Curriculum for England,* DfEE/QCA 1999)

How can we teach citizenship in schools?

It is likely that most provision will fall into three broad models or a combination of these three. The three models are:

1. Citizenship within current core and foundation curriculum

- Citizenship is 'embedded' in 'other' subjects.
- Responsibility for coordination given to specific department, for example, Humanities.
- Citizenship likely to be taught by range of subject specialists, not 'citizenship' specialists.

2. Citizenship within PHSE and/'Citizenship' lessons
- Citizenship curriculum takes place within discrete 'citizenship' lessons.
- Citizenship teaching and learning will draw on the National Curriculum.
- Citizenship likely to be taught by PHSE specialists.

3. Citizenship within whole school
- Citizenship is essential part of whole-school ethos.
- School has close links with community.
- School (pupils and staff) has identity as 'community of learners'.
- Citizenship curriculum occurs *throughout* National Curriculum. Special events or 'citizenship days' are integral to the curriculum, not 'bolt on'.

It is likely and I believe desirable that, over time, schools may move towards the third model. However, whichever model or combination of models is followed, there are certain issues and challenges that need to be addressed. For example:

- How will pupils know they are learning citizenship?
- How will a range of teachers coordinate their planning for teaching and learning in citizenship?
- How do teachers assess progression and achievement in citizenship?
- What does progression in citizenship – participation, discussion, reflection, responsibility – look like?
- How can teachers assess an area of learning that is to do with values, beliefs and attitudes?
- How can teachers work with community partners to plan and assess citizenship?
- How can assessment in citizenship be manageable given its whole-school aspects?

It is these issues and challenges that inspections by Ofsted will set out to evaluate with regard to citizenship.

How will this book help?

This book supports all three models and addresses the challenges set out above in the following ways.

Planning for teaching and learning in citizenship

In this book, each activity begins with a set of **Learning Objectives**. *All* learning objectives are expressed in pupil language. Whichever of the three models outlined above or combination of them is adopted, pupils will need to know when and how they are learning citizenship. In this way, the potential dangers of 'embedding' citizenship (and therefore of it disappearing altogether at the same time!) can be overcome. It is good practice to share learning objectives with pupils so that they:

- Know when learning in citizenship is happening.
- Understand what learning is expected of them and why.
- Appreciate 'the point' of their learning.
- Are able to use alternative learning routes, where needed, to achieve the same objectives.
- Are better able to manage and improve on their own progress.

Sharing learning objectives with pupils also supports assessment. The effectiveness of teacher assessment and feedback is highly dependant on the clarity of learning objectives and pupil understanding of what they are doing and why.

If model 1 or 3 is used teachers will need to combine or integrate 'citizenship learning objectives' with learning objectives from across the National Curriculum. For example, a history topic on the franchise/development of parliament would have both history and citizenship learning objectives. The pupils would need to know this and, at some point, their learning in history for citizenship would need to be applied within another context, for example, school council, drama about power in the community, interviews with councillors, debate about British democracy.

Teachers can use the learning objectives in this book to write their own learning outcomes and assessment criteria. Pupils can use the learning objectives to build up their own portfolio or Record of Achievement in citizenship education.

Each activity in the book has a section called **Curriculum Links**, which sets out each subject area (including Literacy and Numeracy) that is directly relevant to the activity. This section enables schools to either plan for citizenship within particular curriculum areas (as in models 1 and 3 above) or to identify links between citizenship and National Curriculum subjects (as in model 2 above).

The section **Curriculum Links** also indicates simply and clearly where there are opportunities for different curriculum areas to collaborate to plan cross-curricular projects in citizenship. Almost all of the activities in the book could be taught as cross-curricular activities.

The areas of knowledge, understanding and skills covered by Chapters 1 to 6 can be used to plan a citizenship curriculum which:

- Covers the three main strands of citizenship as defined in the programme of study, that is
  (i) social and moral responsibility
  (ii) community involvement
  (iii) political literacy.
- Enables pupils to become informed and responsible citizens while taking action as citizens. Each activity has a participatory element and the section **Taking Community Action!** gives opportunities to build on activities so that pupils can use their knowledge, understanding and skills to take positive action as citizens in the community.

The **Taking Community Action!** section also gives ideas and, in some cases, exemplifies good practice in community projects, including the 'one off special' events which some schools may use to target citizenship. In addition, there are many examples of how teachers can work with community partners to provide citizenship education. Appendix B shows how community partners can also act as assessors of achievements and progression in citizenship.

Assessing progress and achievement in citizenship

What will it look like if a pupil gets better at citizenship? How can we enable this progress to happen? How will we know when it does?

For many teachers, the idea of assessing citizenship – an area of learning that is to do with values, beliefs, attitudes – is a cause of anxiety. In addition, many teachers are not experienced in assessing progress in the central aspects of citizenship, for example, participation, reflection, discussion, responsibility. Questions such as 'precisely how does progress in "reflection" or "discussion" take place?' will arise.

This book enables teachers to overcome these concerns by offering models of progress in these areas (see Appendix A). This appendix also contains models for enabling pupils to reflect on their own values, beliefs and attitudes. It is this quality of reflection that is the key to assessing these areas of the citizenship curriculum. For example, pupils who recognise that, firstly, they had racist values, secondly, that knowledge and understanding about ethnic minorities changed these values, are making great progress in citizenship.

How can pupils assess their own progress and achievements?

Self assessment is an important tool within citizenship learning. Self assessment helps pupils reflect, gain self-knowledge and better manage their own progress. In addition, it can make assessment more manageable for schools by placing some responsibility on pupils. Appendix B contains models for using both self assessment and peer assessment with pupils. Pupils who are practised at making effective self assessments are also better able to manage portfolios and records of achievement.

Useful Contacts

The Useful Contacts section at the end of the book lists organisations and their contact details which may be useful for a particular activity. They are organised by chapter.

Resource Pages

These are designed for pupils and support the activities in the book. They can be photocopied or displayed as OHTs. Teachers may wish to adapt them for the needs of particular groups or individuals. These pages are free of any restrictions of copyright.

1 Identity and Belonging

About this chapter

This chapter focuses on the key areas of identity and belonging. All pupils investigate their identity and the cultural, social, political, regional and religious groups that they belong to. At first the focus is on personal identity and then on the different groups and communities to which the pupils belong. They use a range of sources including information and communication technology (ICT) to find out about their family history. The idea of difference and of cultural diversity as a cause for celebration is raised. The focus then moves on to look at the question of British national identity. Pupils find out about ethnic diversity in Britain since prehistoric times and about the legal changes in British citizenship between 1945 and the present day. They use this knowledge and understanding to reflect on and debate the nature of being 'British'.

Note: There may be particular areas of sensitivity for those who have no knowledge of their personal family history in Section 3 below. Strategies to deal with this are suggested in the Section. In addition, there may be some pupils in some schools (refugees, asylum seekers, 'transits') who do not think of themselves as British. However, everyone will have some understanding of what it means to be British because they are currently living here and this should not prevent them from participating fully in all the learning.

1. Who am I?

Activity A: Who am I?

Target Group: Year 7

Learning Objectives
I should learn:

- About 'Who I am?' 'Where do I belong?' 'How am I different to others?'
- How and why differences are a cause for celebration.

- To recognise and name some of the groups to which I belong.
- To express 'Who I am?' 'Where do I belong?' in a work of art.

Curriculum Links
History: Personal identity, diversity, personal, family and local history.
Geography: Communities and belonging. Regional diversity. Using maps.
Languages: Modern, European and home languages. National and European identity.

Individually, ask students to create a *'Who am I?'* spider diagram, by brainstorming all the characteristics that make them an individual, e.g. I have red hair, I wear spectacles, I am really good at writing but not so good at maths, Pizza is my favourite food, I go to church, I speak Turkish at home and English at school, I am the oldest in my family, I have two stepbrothers and so on.

Individually, ask pupils to use photographs, drawings, magazine cuttings, etc., to make a collage that shows their ideas about *'Who am I?'* They can add words and sentences in different languages. For example, if the activity is being done as part of French, they could write in French or use their home languages as appropriate.

Discuss the different groups/communities to which the pupils belong. These could be very varied and include ethnic, religious, regional, national, related to age, gender, interests, disability/impairment, second families, etc.

Discuss how pupils could make images about their own groups/communities. They could use photographs, newspaper cuttings. They could design symbols or use existing ones to represent different groups/communities, for example, flags, emblems, mottos, icons, coats of arms.

1. Pupils make their own collage.
2. Ask pupils to present their collage to the class, explaining their images and the ideas behind them.
3. Display all the pupils' collages and use to identify similarities and differences.
4. Use the presentations or the display to discuss:
   (a) In what ways are we all different to each other?
   (b) Why is it good that we are different?
   (c) Why is it important to think about 'identity' (who I am) and 'belonging'?
5. Discuss how being different can also be a problem. Use the collages to highlight characteristics that people might pick on them for. Talk about how being teased might make someone feel and how this behaviour could be challenged assertively.
6. Some pupils may make links between the characteristics they have identified about themselves and the communities to which they belong. For example, I enjoy Sunday school and I belong to the Catholic Church; I speak Turkish at home and English at school because I am British and my ethnic origin is Turkish.

Taking Community Action!
Ask pupils how they felt about coming to secondary school.

What thoughts and anxieties did they have about 'fitting in'? How might it have helped to know all the different sorts of people at secondary school?

In groups/as a class, **design a brochure for Year 6 children** in feeder primary schools. The brochure should show them all the different identities at school and the different groups they belong to. The purpose of the brochure is to give information, to welcome and to reassure Year 6.

2. Who are the British?

Activity A: Who are the British?

Target Group: Years 8 to 9

Learning Objectives
I should learn:

- That the British are made up of different ethnic groups.
- That these different groups have been moving into and settling in Britain since prehistoric times.
- How different groups have made important contributions to British life and culture.
- To take part in a discussion.
- To use what I have found out to think about and discuss 'What does it mean to be British?'

Curriculum Links
History: Migration and settlement in British history. Identity and diversity.
Languages: Origin and development of English and other languages spoken by the British.
Literacy: Development and use of language.

The boxes in Resource 1: Activity A: Who are the British? give information about some of the groups of people who have migrated to and settled in Britain over time. The first task is to match up each description with the correct ethnic group. *Either* Pupils can be given cards (30 in total) and asked to 'find their partner'; *or* each pupil can be given a copy of the cards and asked to match them up. Useful resources that pupils can use to work out the correct answers include world maps, ICT – websites and CD-ROMs, history, geography and religious education textbooks.

In pairs or small groups, talk about:

- How easy was it to match up the pairs?
- What was interesting to them? Why?

- What new information did they learn?
- Did they disagree with anything on the cards? If so, what?

What have they learnt from this exercise about the question:

- 'What does it mean to be British'?

For example, does it mean you have to be born here? Does it mean your grand-parents have to be born here? Does it mean what colour you are? Does it mean what religion you are? Does it mean you have to live here? Does it mean you have to be a royalist? Does it mean you have to have a British passport? Does it mean you have to feel British? Does it mean you have to always agree with the British government? Does it mean you have to want to be British? What other ideas do you have about what it means to be British?

Write definitions of what it means to be British. They could start like this: 'A British person is someone who . . .'

Display the definitions. Which ones do all pupils agree with?

Key words

Refugee A person who leaves their country because of persecution due to race, religion, political beliefs, nationality, membership of a group.

Asylum seeker A person who has asked for sanctuary in a country because they are a refugee.

Answers to Resource 1: Activity A: Who are the British?

A Angles, Saxons, Jutes
B Roma Gypsies
C Celts
D Irish
E Afghans
F Kosovan Albanians
G Bangladeshi
H African Caribbean
I Jews
J Chinese
K Indians
L Normans
M French Huguenots
N Italians
O West Africans

Resource 1: Activity A: Who are the British?

Celts	Roma Gypsies	West Africans
Chinese	Afghans	Angles, Saxons, Jutes
Normans	French Huguenots	Italians
Kosovan Albanians	Indians	Jews
African Caribbean	Bangladeshi	Irish

Resource 1 (continued)

A. They came to Britain from northern Europe in the 5th and 6th centuries. Some stayed in Europe and settled there. Some were invited to come to Britain by Celts to help fight against the Picts who were raiding Britain from the area that is Scotland today. However, they then themselves pushed the Celts into the north and west of Britain. Today one fifth of the English language is based on their language.	**B.** These people came from India to Europe in the 14th century. They started to settle in Britain in Tudor times. Other groups have very often persecuted them. Large numbers were murdered by Nazis in the middle of the 20th century and in the Balkans, including Serbia, at the end of the 20th century. Some are famous for their skills with horses. Today they are the largest and poorest minority in Europe.	**C.** They came to Britain from Europe before the 1st century BC. The Angles, Saxons and Jutes pushed many of them into Wales, Scotland and Cornwall. They made beautiful jewellery and pots. Today in Wales many people speak Welsh, which is based on their language.
D. They came to Britain in large numbers in the 19th century. Most came to build roads, railways and canals and do other jobs that the British would not do. Some were also escaping a terrible famine in the 1840s that killed about 2 million. Many also came in the 1950s and 1960s because Britain was short of workers. They are the largest ethnic minority group in Britain today.	**E.** They came to Britain from Asia as refugees from 1972 onwards when the USSR invaded their country. They continue to have to leave their country in the early 21st century and are the biggest refugee group in Britain today. They were and still are escaping war, famine, persecution, torture and other abuses of human rights. Most of them are Muslim.	**F.** They came to Britain from eastern Europe (the Balkans) as refugees in the late 20th century and early 21st century. In the 1990s many were escaping mass murders of their ethnic group in their own country.
G. They came from a country in Asia that was known as East Pakistan up to 1971. Many came in the 1960s and 1970s and set up businesses, including restaurants and textile (cloth) workshops. Their part of Asia had been in the British Empire and they had the same rights as British citizens. Their main religion is Islam. They speak many languages including Bengali, English and Sylheti.	**H.** They came from islands near the Americas that are now a popular holiday place. At first they were taken to those islands by force as slaves from Africa. They were made to work growing sugar and tobacco. After World War 2 many came to Britain because Britain was short of workers. Also their countries had been in the British Empire and they had the same rights as British citizens. They speak English and their main religion is Christianity.	**I.** These people came to Britain from Europe from the Middle Ages onwards. However, they were persecuted and made to leave Britain in 1290. Cromwell let them back in the 17th century. They have often been persecuted across Europe. About 5 million were killed by Nazis in the Holocaust. Many came to Britain in the late 19th and 20th century as refugees.
J. These people came to Britain from Asia in the 1950s and 1960s. Many worked in the hotel and catering trade setting up their own restaurants throughout Britain. Towards the end of the 20th century and start of the 21st, many came as refugees escaping abuses of human rights. Today many are being tortured and executed for criticising their rulers. They speak English, Cantonese, Hakka, Mandarin. Their religions include Buddhism, Taoism, Confucianism, Christianity.	**K.** Most came to Britain in the 1950s and 1960s although many had come earlier and from the time when their country became a British colony. From 1773 one of their foods, curry, started to appear on British menus. Those who came in the 1950s and 1960s came because Britain was short of workers. They worked in the food industry, textile (cloth) industry and took jobs many British people did not want, such as shift work. Many were Sikhs from the Punjab as well as Hindus and Muslims.	**L.** These people came to Britain from northern France in the 11th century. In 1066 their leader, William, defeated (beat) the Anglo Saxons in battle and was crowned king of England. After the victory, they built castles to keep their power. They also took over land and possessions of rich and powerful Anglo Saxons. They spoke French. Modern-day English has many words that come from their language, for example, parliament, furious.
M. About 100,000 came to Britain from western Europe in the 17th century. They were escaping religious persecution in their own country. For example, they were tortured and murdered because of their religion. They came, therefore, as refugees. Most settled in the East End of London and worked in the silk industry.	**N.** These people came to Britain from Europe from the 19th century onwards. Most came to work and make money. They have been very important to the food industry in Britain. Words such as 'opera', 'stiletto', 'balcony' come from their language.	**O.** Many of these people were brought by force to Britain during the 17th and 18th centuries as slaves. By 1787 there were up to 20,000 living in London. Some had arrived even earlier in about 50 AD because they were part of the Roman Empire. A few helped to build Hadrian's Wall between Scotland and Roman England. Today some come to escape abuses of human rights in their own countries. For example, some have been tortured and executed for criticising their rulers.

Note: This activity is based on one in *Multicultural Britain* by J. Cloake and M. R. Tudor, Oxford University Press 2001 and on an activity 'Being British' National Youth Agency 1997, which is now out of print.

Activity B: Why have people come to Britain?

Target Group: Year 8

Learning Objectives
I should learn:

- Why different groups have come to Britain.
- That there are different reasons for migration.

Curriculum Links
History: Migration and settlement in British history. Identity and diversity.

In groups, pupils sort and match cards (i.e. Celts, Roma Gypsies, etc., see Resource 1) to the following headings:

TO BE SAFE	TO WORK
TO CONQUER	TO SETTLE
OTHER?	

What do they notice about the outcomes?

It is likely that some cards will go in more than one column. Why?

Which cards, if any, were in the 'other' column?

Talk about the following *statements*. Do they agree or disagree with each statement? Encourage pupils to use the information on their cards to back up their opinions and conclusions.

- The British have all been immigrants at one time.
- Groups of people have always moved around the world.
- Britain is richer in all sorts of ways because of migration.
- Refugees have often come to Britain to be safe.
- Britain has been a place of safety *and* of persecution.

Activity C: Have people moved out of Britain too? Why?

Target Group: Year 8

Learning Objectives
I should learn:

- That people have also migrated out of Britain.
- That some have left Britain as refugees from persecution and famine.
- How to find out what people think and know.

Curriculum Links
History: Migration and settlement in British history. Identity and diversity.
English Literature: British poetry. Identity and diversity in literature.

(i) In the mid and late twentieth century many people also left Britain, mainly to go to Australia, New Zealand, Canada and South Africa.
Discuss why they might have left Britain.
(ii) From the seventeenth to nineteenth centuries many religious people such as Quakers, Methodists, Baptists also left Britain for America.
Discuss why they might have left Britain.
(iii) From their history lessons, can the pupils think of other groups who have left Britain and why?
For example, Catholics in sixteenth and seventeenth centuries, Irish in nineteenth, Welsh in nineteenth.

How can poetry and fiction express ideas and feelings about identity?
Read poetry or fiction by Benjamin Zephaniah. For example: Poem 'The British' and 'We are British!' by Benjamin Zephaniah, published by Frances Lincoln, £10.99. The latter is a book about 12 children from all over Britain and from a range of cultural backgrounds.

What do people think and know about ethnic diversity in Britain?
- Ask friends, family, other pupils: What percentage of British people today are classified as 'ethnic minorities'?
(The figure in January 2002 was 7.1 per cent but when asked in a nationwide survey most people thought it was higher. You could use the public information website (*www.statistics.gov.uk*) to find out other information.)
- How many answers were right? Too low? Too high?
- Suggest reasons why many people think the percentage of ethnic minorities in Britain is higher than it really is?
- Why do you think it might be important to know the correct figure?
- Which of the 15 ethnic groups in Resource 1 (see Activity A) are no longer classed as ethnic minorities?

There is an opportunity here to use the 'media analysis' activity in Chapter 6 to investigate how newspapers portray ethnic diversity in Britain.

Taking Community Action!

- The card-matching exercise (Activity A, Resource 1) only covers some of the different groups who have migrated into Britain over time. Use Zephaniah's poem to think of others and research their histories. Make a display that will help all the pupils and teachers in your school understand 'Who are the British?'
- Use the information on the cards to write a school quiz. The aim is to give information in a fun and interesting way.

3. Where have my family come from?

Activity A: Asking questions about my family

Target Group: Year 8

Learning Objectives
I should learn:

- About my personal family history.
- How to research family and local history.
- How to use ICT and other sources of information.
- To make my own family tree.

Note: Some pupils may not know who their own family are. In these cases you may wish to give them a family to research – your own family, a local family, important/famous family, *or* adapt the activity so that they are using the census and other resources to find out about a particular home address, *or* adapt the activity for the whole class so that the PRO and Commonwealth War Graves Commission websites (see Activity B below) are used to research *change in the local community* rather than family history.

Curriculum Links
History: Investigating family and local history.
ICT: Using websites as a source of information in an enquiry.

Family tree
As homework, ask pupils to ask questions at home to fill in as much of their own family tree as they can. Some pupils will find this challenging and it might be helpful to show an example of a family tree, for example, your own/the royal family.

Possible questions to ask at home are:

- Names of grandparents, great-grandparents, aunts, uncles, etc.
- Dates of births, marriages and deaths.
- Dates of moving from one place to another.

They should also begin to collect artefacts from home to illustrate their completed family tree, such as photos, certificates, letters, etc.

Give maps to pupils whose families have moved around. These could be local street maps, regional, national or world maps depending on need. Ask pupils to use arrows, annotations, photos, etc., to illustrate their maps to show when and where their family has moved around.

Depending on the different family experiences and backgrounds of the pupils, use one or more of the following approaches to do further family research. These approaches can also be adapted for use with other sources of information.

The success of the activity will depend largely on the research skills of the pupils. Stress that they must, firstly, know what they want to find out, secondly, select only the relevant information for their investigation, thirdly, record all relevant information. Pupil research can be supported with a Record Sheet. For example:

- What do I know now?
- What else do I need to find out?
- Where shall I look?
- What have I found out?

Activity B: Using the Census to find out about family history

Every ten years since 1801 (except during the Second World War in 1941) a census has been carried out in Britain. A census is a record of information. Today it records:

- Every household/address.
- Name and surname of each person who lives there.
- Their ages and their sex.
- Their nationality.
- Their relationship to the head of the family, e.g. husband of/wife of/son of/servant of, etc.
- Their job or profession, how they get to work and whether they have their own car.
- How many in the household are unemployed or change jobs often.
- Whether they are single or married or divorced or separated.
- The date of any marriages.
- Their religion.
- Condition of the home, for example, hot water, bathroom, inside toilet.

From 1991, for the first time, the census also records ethnic origin.

In 2002 the Public Record Office launched the census for 1901 online. All the entries for the 1901 census were put on a website which is easy to use. Pupils, on arrival at the site, are asked to enter the year and the address they are searching for. The census online can be found at the website of the Public Record Office at *www.pro.gov.uk* (the PRO telephone number is 020 8876 3444). The website has a free area as well as a subscription area. Part of the free area includes an exhibition about the census and life in 1901. Copies of all the censuses are also kept at local public record offices.

Activity C: Finding out about your family in war time

There is often more information made and kept about people during war than during peacetime. The Commonwealth War Graves Commission website is an excellent resource to use to find out about any servicemen and women from commonwealth countries, e.g. Jamaica, India, Nigeria, New Zealand, Britain listed on memorials to the First or Second World Wars.

When pupils arrive at the site, it will ask for information including surname, initials, the war fought in, year of death, regiment, force, nationality. They do not need all of this information in order to have a successful search and result. The Commission website will then give as much information as it can about a relative.

The Commonwealth War Graves Commission can be found at *www.cwg.org.uk* (telephone 01628 634221).

Activity D: Using street directories to find out about your family history

Street directories are kept at public record offices. They are easy to use and give information on who lived in each house in a particular year.

Activity E: Using the Black and Asian History Map to find out about your family

In 2000 Channel 4 launched a 'Black and Asian History Map' at *www.blackhistorymap.com* or it can also be found through the Channel 4 website. The main aim was to put the history of black and Asian people in the UK on the map, linking to the sites of black history projects all over the UK. The site is interactive, exciting and fairly easy to use. Black history can be searched:

- by place, using a map of the United Kingdom;
- by date, using a timeline;
- by subject, using a list of events, such as the Bristol Bus Boycott of 1963;
- by 'Family Tree', using a collection of personal stories.

Some of the links, however, are not accessible in language or content to Key Stage 3 pupils and some support may be needed.

4. Who is a British citizen?

Activity A: Citizenship in Britain 1948 to 2002

Target Group: Year 9

Learning Objectives
I should learn:

- Different meanings and uses of the words 'citizenship' and 'citizen'.
- How the law about British citizenship has changed over time and why.

Curriculum Links
History: Migration, settlement. Identity and diversity. Citizenship and law. Modern Britain.

Brainstorm and discuss with pupils, the meaning and uses of the word 'citizenship'.

The word 'citizen' can be used in different ways. Within 'citizenship' lessons at school, the word is usually used to mean a person who has rights (e.g. freedom of speech, freedom of movement) and also responsibilities (what they should do in society, e.g. act responsibly to others, respect others). However, 'citizenship' is also about the legal right to belong to a country. Not everyone in Britain has the legal right to be a citizen even if they were born here. Since the end of the last century, there have been big and heated debates in government and the press about British citizenship. This is partly because this period also saw the greatest number of people migrating around the world either seeking sanctuary (a safe place) from danger or looking for work. In 2002, over 250 million people across the world were not living in their country of birth. About 50 million of these are refugees of some kind and about 95 per cent found sanctuary in Africa and Asia. About 5 per cent have found sanctuary in Europe. This is partly because many refugees stay close to their home country in the hope of returning one day. Most wars and conflicts are in Asia and Africa, not Europe. However, the Balkans conflicts of the 1980s and 1990s partly explain the increase in refugees in Europe.

Give pupils copies of Resource 2.

Discuss the changes and pupils answer the questions at the bottom of Resource 2.

Resource 2: Activity A: Citizenship in Britain 1948 to 2002

Who is a British Citizen?

The question of 'who is a British citizen?' has been changed over time by the law. There have been many different reasons for these changes. In 1945 the Second World War ended. Millions of people had become refugees because of the war. When Soviet Russia began taking over countries in Eastern Europe, there were even more refugees. Many of them, especially from Eastern Europe, came to live in Britain. At this time the British Empire and British Commonwealth was very large. One quarter of the world's population lived within it! All the people who lived within the Empire and Commonwealth had the right to come and live in Britain. After 1945, and because of the postwar changes, the Government began to debate the need for laws about citizenship.

Changes in British Citizenship 1948 to 2002

Date of change	What happened?	Why?
1948	**British Nationality Act.** Gave rights of British citizenship to *all* people living in British Empire and Commonwealth (e.g. India, Nigeria, Canada, Jamaica, Barbados, New Zealand, Kenya, Australia). These rights were equal rights with people born in Britain. Passed by Labour government.	One important reason was that Britain was short of workers, especially to do poorly paid, dirty and inconvenient jobs like shift work, factory work, unskilled work, cleaning, catering, etc. Britain was also short of nurses.
1962	**Immigration Act.** Said black people, including black Asian people, had to have employment voucher before entering Britain. An employment voucher had to prove they had a job or had special skills or qualifications that Britain needed. The number of vouchers was limited. Irish and other white ethnic groups did not need vouchers. Passed by Conservative government.	Britain was no longer short of workers. In addition, it became clear in the 1950s that much of British culture was racist. One 'solution' to these problems was to cut down on the number of black people entering Britain.
1968	**Commonwealth Immigration Act.** Said that Kenyan Asians were no longer allowed to come to Britain even though they had British passports. White Kenyans with British passports were still allowed to come. Passed by Labour government.	In the 1960s the leader of Kenya, Jomo Kenyatta, threatened to expel all 'non Africans' from Kenya. Kenya had been a British colony and during British rule many Asian people settled in Kenya. These Asian people were also British citizens. This Act was rushed through parliament in three days after an MP called Enoch Powell made frightening and racist speeches about the consequences of immigration.
1971	**Immigration Act.** Introduced two groups – 'patrials' and 'non patrials' –	Most patrials were white and from countries like Australia or New Zealand.

Resource 2 (continued)

Date of change	What happened?	Why?
1971	both from Commonwealth countries. Patrials had rights to British citizenship but non patrials did not. Patrials were people born in Britain or with a parent, grandparent or great-grandparent born in Britain. Non patrials were not born in Britain and had no such ancestors born in Britain. Passed by Conservative government.	Many people, including some politicians, said the Act was racist and should not be passed. Anti-racist and anti-fascist organisations were against the Act. The ANL demonstration against this Act was the biggest anti-racist demonstration ever held in Britain.
1973	Britain joins **European Economic Community.** Citizens of EEC able to freely enter and work in Britain though they did not automatically become British citizens.	After the end of the British Empire, Britain had more contact and especially trade (buying and selling) with continental Europe. British people also went on holiday more to Europe.
1981	**British Nationality Act.** Took away rights of citizenship from 'British Nationals'. These were people born in an ex-British colony. Instead only people born to British parents either at home or abroad were British citizens.	During the 1970s, 1980s and 1990s there were important changes into who had rights to come to Britain and rights of citizenship. This was partly because of closer relationship with continental Europe and partly because of increasing restrictions on immigration from the British Commonwealth.

Questions

(i) Make a timeline that shows 'Changes in British Citizenship' 1945 to 2000.
(ii) What different things do you notice about the changes in the law shown above?
(iii) Why do you think the 1962 Immigration Act has been called a 'racist act'?
(iv) How else could the problem of British racism have been tackled?
(v) Write at least one statement about what you have learnt about British citizenship over time.

Activity B: A test for British citizenship?

Target Group: Year 9

Learning Objectives
I should learn:

- Why some politicians and groups want to have a 'citizenship test'.
- Why some politicians and groups oppose (against) a 'citizenship test'.
- About the challenges of living in an ethnically diverse society.
- Using newspapers to find out about beliefs and attitudes.

Curriculum Links
History: Cultural diversity, citizenship and the law, migration and settlement, using newspapers to investigate beliefs and attitudes.

Ask pupils what they think is meant by a 'citizenship test'. Use Resource 3 to examine the issues around citizenship tests. The newspaper extracts show the range of views about citizenship in Britain.

Resource 3: Activity B: A test for British citizenship?

'Migrants must learn to be British'

was the headline of an article in the *Daily Mail* on 7 February 2002. The article was about the Government's suggestions for a new law on citizenship or what has been called a 'citizenship test'. This was not a new idea. In 1990 a politician called Norman Tebbit said it would be an 'interesting test' to know how many British Asians supported cricket teams from their country of ethnic origin (such as India, Bangladesh or Pakistan) rather than supporting British cricket teams. Some people said that Tebbit's idea for a 'test' was racist. They said it was racist because it was suggesting that British Asians were not really 'British' and not really loyal to Britain. Some countries, like the USA, already have 'citizenship tests'.

What did the Government suggest in February 2002?

The Government suggested a new law for immigrants, which became known as the 'Citizenship test'. Immigrants would have to go to citizenship classes to learn about 'being British', that is British values (what is important to the British way of life) and democracy. They would have to promise to adopt British values and protect British democracy (see Chapter 4 for more on democracy). They would have to take part in ceremonies swearing loyalty to the Queen. They would also have to be able to speak basic English. The Government also suggested that it would be better for British people to choose their marriage partner from Britain rather than Asia.

What are the arguments for and against a citizenship test?

While some people supported the idea of a citizenship test others were against it. Many different criticisms were made. For example, some people said that if the Government truly wanted to develop British unity and identity, they would not support segregated schools, such as Catholic, Church of England, Jewish and Islamic schools. In 2002, some people were particularly angry about the comments made about arranged marriages. They said the 'real' reason for the suggestion that it would be better for British people to choose their marriage partner from Britain rather than Asia was *not* because of developing British unity and identity but because of other reasons. These other reasons were to do with trying to cut down on the numbers of people immigrating to Britain. The number of husbands and wives entering Britain from the Asian sub-continent (India, Pakistan, Bangladesh) had been slowly rising. Marriage to a British citizen, after some time, gave these husbands and wives from Asia rights to British citizenship. These people were saying, therefore, that the Government had a *'hidden agenda'*. A 'hidden agenda' is when someone says they want to do something for a reason but actually the real reason is very different.

Read the sources below. One is for a citizenship test and one is against.

> **Source A**
>
> The recent media hoo-ha about citizenship has not focused on all people only certain kinds. The question of citizenship has slipped into that other familiar question – can Britain's minority communities ever be part of the nation.
> *Dr Gargi Battacharya, Lecturer in Politics & Religion, University of Birmingham, in the* Guardian, *21 February 2002*

Resource 3 (continued)

Source B

Vital asset
THIS country needs new blood if it is to survive and prosper.
As the birth rate drops, our workforce is shrinking.
We need new people who will work hard – often doing jobs we don't want to do.
We need new people who want to succeed.
So we should welcome immigrants who want to be British.

They are an asset. They will give us their skills, their sweat and their loyalty.
That is why the *Sun* salutes David Blunkett for his imaginative plans on immigration.

Helping newcomers to learn our language and understand our culture will make them feel welcome – at home, in fact.

The Sun, *8 February 2002*
(David Blunkett is the Home Secretary of the Government and it is his job to look after immigration)

Questions

(i) Which source supports the citizenship test and which does not?
(ii) What is the main point being made in Source A?
(iii) How does Source B back up its opinion of the citizenship test?

Activity C: What do *you* think?

Target Group: Year 9

Learning Objectives
I should learn:

- To reflect on my learning and to form my own opinion.
- That different people in Britain today have different views about citizenship.
- To take part in a discussion.

Curriculum Links
History: Identity and diversity. Politics of race, racism.
Religious Education: Religious and cultural identity and diversity.

Ask the pupils to reflect on what their views are. The opinions expressed by Persons A to C on Resource 4 will stimulate their ideas.

Resource 4: Activity C: What do *you* think?

Read the statements below. In groups sort them into agree/disagree.
You might want to agree some ground rules (see Appendix C to this book) for your discussion.

(i) Now make your own table of 'pro citizenship test' and 'against citizenship test' statements. Use and adapt the statements above to help you.
(ii) Why do *you* think that some British people supported a citizenship test in 2002? What different reasons could they have had?

Taking Community Action!
'Our School Way'
All groups, including communities and institutions, have an identity even if they don't think about it. What identity does your school have? What does it mean to be in your school? What does your school 'stand for'? Make a 'citizenship test' for your school. Call it 'Our School Way'; *or* rather than thinking about how your school actually is, you could think about how you would like it to be. What could your school's identity aim to be?

Design a symbol to reflect your school's identity.

What messages should that symbol send?

5. What does it mean to be British today?

Activity A: What does being British mean to me?

Target Group: Year 9

Learning Objectives
I should learn:

- To think about what it means to be British today.
- To design a symbol to communicate my ideas.
- To use my knowledge and understanding about British history and identity.

Curriculum Links
Art and Design: Using art and design to interpret and use symbols. Expressing beliefs and values through art.
History: British identity. National symbols. Interpretations and representations.

Refer back to all the learning in this unit. Remind pupils about the definitions they reached about being British and some of the reasons why the question of national identity has been a controversial and difficult question.

Look at the illustration showing the Union Flag.

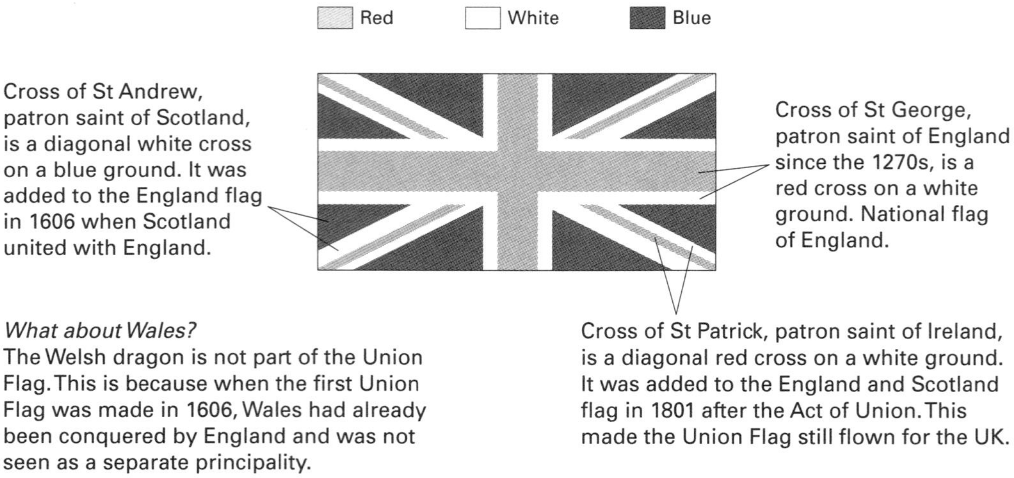

What does the Union Flag mean to you?

Brainstorm all the different symbols that might communicate what it means to be British today. For example, passport, currency, Big Ben, Houses of Parliament, free press, etc.

What does each symbol have to do with what it means to be British today?

Collect emblems, symbols and logos of organisations, groups, nations, or ask pupils to do this as homework. For example, flags, Oxfam, Red Cross, United Nations, McDonalds, banks, businesses, the school, etc. Discuss the different messages sent by different images.

Ask pupils to design their own image that communicates their understanding of what it means to be British. Use the following questions to guide them:

- Is your symbol or poster going to be positive or negative about Britain?
- How do you want people to feel when they look at your symbol or poster? Proud/happy/sad/hopeful/hopeless/important/connected to others/isolated/alone?
- What messages do you want to send about being British?

2 Human Rights for Human Beings

About this chapter

The chapter begins with a focus on rights and responsibilities at school and the importance of trust to respecting the rights of others. Pupils consider the function of rules at school, and laws in the wider society, as being primarily about protecting our rights. They progress to reflecting on the nature of being human and, therefore, of the nature of human rights. They find out about the content and purpose of the United Nations' Universal Declaration of Human Rights, how human rights have been and are being abused in some parts of the world and the organisations and personalities who take positive action for human rights.

1. What are my rights and responsibilities?

Activity A: The importance of trust

Target Group: Year 7

Learning Objectives
I should learn:

- About the meaning of 'rights' and 'responsibilities'.
- About the importance of 'trust' to human rights.
- To act responsibly towards others.
- What it feels like to have to trust someone to take care of me.
- To reflect on what I have learnt.

Curriculum Links
English Literature: Trust and mistrust as common themes in stories and poems.
History: Rights and responsibilities throughout history.

Blindfold half the class. Each pupil in the sighted half chooses a partner from the blindfolded group. There should be no talking while this is done. Ask the sighted group to lead the blindfolded group around the class, school, playground (as appropriate) for about 10 minutes. Explain that:

(i) The leaders must take care of the led so that they are safe throughout.
(ii) At the same time they make sure the blindfolded have as wide a range of experiences as possible, for example, different walking surfaces, touching different objects.

Change over and repeat the activity.

Note: With some classes, you may wish to ask pupils to agree a contract to act responsibly as leaders. If they do not agree, they cannot take part.

Discuss the questions:
How did it feel to be blindfolded? Helpless? Frightening? Free? Younger?
Was it easy or hard to trust the leader? Why? Why not?
How did it feel to be responsible for the 'blind'?
How did it change your behaviour?

Agree a list of **rights** of the blindfolded, for example, 'to be safe'.
Agree a list of **responsibilities** of the leaders, for example, 'to be careful', 'to walk slowly'.

There are opportunities to follow up this activity with work in Literacy and/English Literature. For example:

What stories or poems are being read that are about trust and mistrust? Why are trust and mistrust common topics in stories?

Activity B: What are our rights and responsibilities at school?

Target Group: Year 7

Learning Objectives
I should learn:

- To think about my rights at school.
- To think about my responsibilities or duties at school.
- To begin to understand the relationship between rights and responsibilities.
- In what ways responsibilities are important to rights.
- That 'rules' are usually made to protect the rights of all at school.

Curriculum Links
Religious Education: Rights and responsibilities.
History: Rights and responsibilities throughout history.

Brainstorm as a class **What are our rights and responsibilities at school?** For example:

My rights are:	My responsibilities/duties are:
To be listened to by the teacher To be warm and safe To have regular breaks/rests To be taught the National Curriculum To be respected – not bullied/picked on for any reason, e.g. race, gender, disability	To do my homework on time To work quietly when asked To take part when asked To respect others

When the lists are complete (similar to as shown in the above example), ask pupils to make links between rights and responsibilities, for example 'to be respected' and 'to respect others'.
Ask the pupils to think of statements that explain the relationship between rights and responsibilities. For example, 'I cannot have all my rights if others do not act responsibly'.

Which rights are written down somewhere in the school? Why is it important to have 'school policies' or rights?
Which rights are not written down? What do they notice about the differences? Why are some written down but not all?
To stimulate pupils' ideas about this question, it might be helpful to ask:

> What if a new pupil arrived from the planet Mars – why might *all* rights and responsibilities need to be written down for them?
> How is 'trust' important to rights and responsibilities?

Are responsibilities/duties the same as 'rules'? Why are there 'rules' at school? Which ones protect pupil rights?

At this point you may wish to anticipate 'Law, Justice and Crime' (Chapter 3) by discussing laws as being rules for the whole community.

> How does it feel when rights are ignored or trampled on? For example, if we are picked on because of the way we are? Or if we are bullied?
> Why is it important to act responsibly?
> Why is it important to listen to others? To respect others?

Ask the pupils to think about:

> Do teachers have rights and responsibilities too? Write lists of 'Teacher Rights and Responsibilities'.

Which rules at your school protect teacher rights?
Who else protects teacher rights? Unions? General Teaching Council? DfES?
Who else protects children's rights? NSPCC? Social Services? Children's Society?

Taking Community Action!

(i) Review and reflect on school policies:
   - Are they in pupil language?
   - Do all pupils know about them?

(ii) Make posters to illustrate/advertise/spread awareness of rights or responsibilities. For example, 'right to get my lunch peacefully'/'responsibility not to push in' near food queue in canteen. Put them in appropriate places.

(iii) Make a 'School Rights' display.

Activity C: What does it mean to be human?

Target Group: Year 7

Learning Objectives
I should learn:

- What it means to be human.
- What humans have in common.

Curriculum Links
Religious Education: Nature of being human. Rights and responsibilities.
History: Rights and responsibilities throughout history. Abuses of human rights, including slavery, gender and economic inequality.

Teacher uses 'hot seating' (going into role as an individual) to discuss what it means to be human. Teacher hot seats as someone just arrived from the planet Mars. You are not human but – fortunately – can speak English. Ask the pupils:

- I have never seen things like you before. What are you?

Clearly you will need to respond flexibly but useful prompts/questions to prepare yourself for might include:

- What does this word 'human' mean?
- What makes you human?
- Is that chair also human? Why not?
- What do you have that the chair doesn't?
- Is that bird also human? Why not?
- What do you have that that bird doesn't?

Teachers may want to use learning in history to extend this activity to look at the consequences of not being seen as fully human. In the past, not everyone was thought of as fully or properly human. Some people have been seen as less human than others. For example, aborigines in Australia, African slaves in the seventeenth to eighteenth century, women in some societies, children in some societies, poor people, the mentally ill and so on. Seeing others as less human (than they are) has enabled some people to treat others badly.

- What examples, from their history lessons, can pupils think of when some people have been treated as 'less human' than others?
- What are the consequences of being seen as or of seeing others as 'less than human'?

2. What are human rights? Do all people have them?

Activity A: Making rules for our world

Target Group: Year 8

Learning Objectives
I should learn:

- That human rights are to do with fairness and equality for all.
- To think about different systems of government and rights.

Curriculum Links
History: Different systems of government, power, rulers, laws and rights.
English Literature/Literacy: Stories about power and government, for example, *Animal Farm* by George Orwell.
Drama: Using imagination and fantasy to explore learning.

Refer back to Activity C in Section 1 above. Ask the pupils why it is important to recognise that all peoples are human. Suggest that it is important because everyone who is human has a right to 'human rights'.

Ask pupils, in small groups, to make rules or laws for their own world. However, they do not know who they will be in this world – poor, rich, black, white, male, female, young, old, healthy, sick, sensory impaired, able bodied, etc. They should decide:

- Who should rule (small group, one person, everyone)?
- Who should chose rulers?
- What rights should people have?

Pupils may want to think about money, food, work, health, education, etc.

- What responsibilities and duties will people have/what will everyone have to do?

Talk about the 'pupil worlds'.

- Was anyone left out of some rights?
- Were the worlds 'fair' or 'unfair'? In what ways?
- Did people have 'equal rights' or not?
- What difference did it make not to know 'who' you might be?

Activity B: What is a dictatorship?

Target Group: Year 8

Learning Objectives
I should learn:

- What it means to live in a dictatorship.
- What is a 'dictator' and how they can behave.
- That a dictatorship does not respect human rights.
- Why it is important to say what human rights should be.

Curriculum Links
History: Systems of government, including dictatorships. Civil rights in the USA, Ireland.

Depending on your style as a teacher, the nature of your pupils and your relationship with them, you may wish to vary the approach to this activity by either being the dictator yourself or inviting pupils to take turns as the dictator. You may wish to do the activity 'cold' – that is surprise them by suddenly behaving like a dictator.
Pupil/teacher takes on role of dictator for 5 to 10 minutes. The dictator must give instructions during the lesson and everyone must obey them. For example:

- Answer 'yes' to every question.
- Stand up.
- Hum all the time.
- Sit on your hands.
- Believe everything I say.
- Bow to me.
- Call me 'Oh Great One' when you speak to me.

The dictator could pick on some pupils and favour others.

Questions
(i) How did the pupils feel when treated in this way?
(ii) How could the pupils have used their rights at school to challenge the way 'the dictator' acted?
(iii) What feelings might people have who really live in dictatorships?
(iv) What dictatorships – today and in the past – can the pupils think of?

3. What is the Universal Declaration of Human Rights? What are the challenges for human rights in the world today?

Activity A: Human rights are for human beings!

Target Group: Years 8 to 9

Learning Objectives
I should learn:

- Why the Universal Declaration of Human Rights was written in 1948.
- What it says in the Universal Declaration of Human Rights.
- That abuses of human rights have happened under different political systems.
- That many people and organisations fight for better human rights.

Curriculum Links
History: Historical background to the Universal Declaration of Human Rights. Dictatorships, fascism, nazism, the Holocaust, genocide, rights and responsibilities.
Religious Education: Nature of being human and the Holocaust.

Note: Pupils in Year 8 are unlikely to have studied dictatorships yet as part of their history curriculum. The paragraph below gives a brief outline of the historical background to the Universal Declaration of Human Rights. Either use the paragraph to build your own resources or photocopy it for pupils.

Historical background to the Universal Declaration of Human Rights

The Universal Declaration of Human Rights was written in 1948 after the Second World War. During the Second World War, over five million Jews were murdered in the Holocaust. Other groups, including gypsies, Slavs, disabled people, the mentally ill, homosexuals, were also victims of mass murder by Nazi Germany. There were other horrors happening in the world. In Soviet Russia, for example, over ten million people had lost their lives through Stalin's policies to modernise Russia. Between 1945 and 1948, countries in Eastern Europe, such as, Poland, Romania, Bulgaria, Albania, were being taken over by communist USSR. Citizens of communist countries were not allowed to leave their country, speak freely, meet freely, newspapers were tightly controlled. This system of dictatorship was similar to that of Hitler in Nazi Germany.

The Declaration, therefore, was – in part – a direct consequence and response to the particular horrors of the 1930s and 1940s. It was also the product of a Western, democratic and capitalist political, social and cultural mindset of Western, capitalist, liberal democracies. However, it is important that pupils understand that abuses of the human rights listed in the Declaration also occur within the Western world. Some, such as famine, inequality and poverty are – in part – consequences of capitalism although they may not be so obvious or easy for us, living within a capitalist world, to recognise.

Questions

(i) Hand out a copy of the Universal Declaration of Human Rights, Resource 5, to each pupil/pair of pupils. Point out that this is not the original language but it has been adapted especially for them. The meaning has not been changed though there is less detail than in the original.

(ii) Compare the rights in the 'pupil worlds' to the Universal Declaration of Human Rights.
  (a) How are they similar and different?

(iii) Point out that the Universal Declaration of Human Rights was written in 1948.
  (a) How many years ago was that?
  (b) In what ways does it leave out important issues of today? For example, environmental issues?
  (c) Make a list of 'Human Rights for Our Environment'. For example, the right to have clean air to breathe, the right not to have the local environment poisoned by dangerous chemicals, etc.

(iv) Are there any other issues that the pupils feel are not covered in the Universal Declaration of Human Rights?

Resource 5: Activity A: Human rights are for human beings

The Universal Declaration of Human Rights

1. All human beings are born free and equal in rights and dignity.	2. Everyone has the right to human rights whatever their colour, sex, nationality, class, etc.	3. Everyone has the right to live in freedom and safety.	4. Nobody should be made a slave.	5. Nobody should be tortured or hurt in a cruel or degrading way as a punishment.
6. Everyone has the right to be protected by laws, wherever they are.	7. Everyone is equal before the law. Laws should be applied fairly and in the same way to everyone.	8. If your rights are abused, you can ask for help.	9. Nobody should be put in prison or sent out of their country unjustly/without a good reason.	10. Anyone put on trial must be tried in public. The judges must not be influenced by others.
11. Everyone should be thought innocent until it is proved that they are guilty. Everyone has the right to defend themselves. Nobody can be punished for something they haven't done.	12. Everyone has the right to privacy. Nobody can enter your home without permission. If someone attacks you, you have the right to be protected.	13. Everyone has the right to move around freely inside their own country. And they have the right to leave and enter their own country.	14. Everyone has the right to find safety (asylum) in another country if they need to. However, you lose this right if you have killed someone or gone against human rights.	15. Everyone has the right to belong to a country and have a nationality. Nobody can stop you from changing your nationality without a good reason.
16. Adults have the right to marry and have children. Nobody can force you to marry.	17. Everyone has the right to own property and nobody can take it away from them.	18. Everyone has the right to choose their own religion and to worship.	19. Everyone has the right to 'freedom of speech' – to think and say what they wish.	20. Everyone has the right to meet together peacefully. Nobody can be forced to join any group.

Resource 5 (continued)

21. Everyone has the right to have a say in government. This should happen through free and secret elections.	22. Everyone has the right to social security and each country must help each individual make the best of themselves.	23. Everyone has the right to work, to choose work and to have good conditions at work. Everyone has the right to equal pay for equal work. Everyone can join a union or group to protect themselves at work.	24. Everyone has the right to rest and leisure, including paid holidays.	25. Everyone has the right to a healthy standard of living. This includes food, water, housing, medical care and security when old or sick. Mothers and children should have special care.
26. Everyone has the right to go to school and get an education. Parents have the right to choose education for their children. All education should aim to develop the whole child and promote peace in the world and respect for all.	27. Everyone has the right to take part and contribute to cultural life, including art, literature, science, drama.	28. Everyone should be able to enjoy their rights and to have their rights protected throughout the world. There must be, therefore, a world 'order' which upholds and protects human rights.	29. Everyone also has responsibilities and duties towards others. Laws must be made to protect rights and uphold responsibilities and duties.	30. No person, group or country can do anything to destroy the rights in this declaration.

Activity B: Do all people have their human rights?

Target Group: Years 8 to 9

Learning Objectives
I should learn:

- How the rights of some people have been and are being abused.
- How individuals and organisations have fought for human rights.
- How to use the Universal Declaration of Human Rights to challenge abuses of human rights in the world.
- Use of newspapers to analyse values (what people think is important), beliefs, attitudes to rights and abuses of rights.

Curriculum Links
History: Rights and abuses of rights, political systems including dictatorships. Resistance, activism and role of the individual.
Literacy: Writing concisely and precisely, summarising information for a particular audience.
ICT: Using ICT websites as sources of information.

(i) Discuss the meaning of 'universal declaration'. Does this mean all rights are respected everywhere in the world? Resource 6 'Abuses of human rights' are all real situations that have happened since 1948 or are happening in the world today.
Give each pupil/pair a copy.
(ii) According to the Universal Declaration of Human Rights, which human right or rights does each 'abuse'?
Ask pupils to match abuses to rights.
(iii) Bring in a range of daily newspapers. In groups/pairs ask pupils to find items that are, in some way, to do with human rights.
Ask pupils to select one item each and give a short presentation outlining:
  - What is the item about? Which newspaper?
  - What does it have to do with human rights?
  - Any other important or interesting points?

Resource 6: Activity B: Do all people have their human rights?

Abuses of human rights

Internment in Northern Ireland

In 1971 the British government introduced 'internment' in Northern Ireland. 'Internment' meant that terrorist suspects could be put in prison without being charged with a crime or put on trial. On 9 August 1971, 342 'suspects' were arrested and locked up. 340 were Catholic and 2 were Protestant. Edward Heath, Prime Minister of Britain, said internment was needed to make the UK a safer place. However, it failed to do this. There was more violence and rioting in Northern Ireland. The IRA became more popular. This was partly because internment was very one sided. Only two Protestants were arrested, the rest were Catholic. Many Catholics said this proved that Britain was on the side of Protestants. Internment was ended in Northern Ireland in 1974. Between 1971 and 1974 thousands of Catholics and IRA members had been imprisoned without trial.

Death penalty in the world

People can be executed for crimes that threaten property not people, for example robbery, in 87 countries in the world today. During 2000, there were 1,457 official executions in the world. The real figure is probably much higher. 88 per cent of these executions happened in China, Iran, Saudi Arabia and the USA. Seven countries have executed children since 1990. Fourteen of these child executions were in the USA. Prisoners in the USA and UK have been executed and then found to have been innocent. In many countries, most of those executed are poor, ethnic minorities or political opponents of the rulers. The UK last executed someone in 1964 and abolished the death penalty in 1998. Since 1991, about three countries a year have abolished the death penalty. Amnesty International is an organisation that fights for human rights, including an end to the death penalty.

(*Source:* Amnesty International 2002)

Child workers and slavery

The International Labour Organisation said there were around 250 million children working in the world in 2000. About 120 million of these children were working full time and about 70 per cent were slaves getting no pay. Many worked in dangerous conditions, such as mines. They did not go to school. Many of these child workers are victims of 'trafficking'. Trafficking is a type of slavery. Trafficking means to be taken away from your home by force or by using lies. Children are trafficked and used as domestic servants, farm workers and prostitutes. There is child labour, slavery and trafficking throughout the world, including Britain.

Slavery: Bonded labour

There are many different kinds of slavery in the world today. 'Bonded labour' is one type. 'Bonded labour' is when a person sells themselves or their family to repay a loan or debt. They work for little or no pay and many work for seven days a week. Some women and children are used for sex. In 1999 the United Nations said there were more than two million bonded labourers in the world. They work for far more time than they owed in money. They are usually guarded and sometimes kept in chains.

'I became bonded after I got married to my husband 20 years ago – his family had been bonded for three generations to the same landlord – I used to work from 6 a.m. in the landlord's house – cleaning, fetching water . . . Then I would go to work on the farm . . . cutting, threshing and so on until 7 p.m. or later.'

Leelu Bai, former bonded labourer woman from Thane District, India, 1999
(*Source:* Antislavery Organisation 2002)

Resource 6 (continued)

Famine in Sudan and Ethiopia The Sudan and Ethiopia are countries in the horn of Africa or northeast Africa. The Sudan suffered a terrible drought in the mid 1980s. As a result, the crops failed and there was a famine. Less than half the Sudanese people had access to clean water. The situation in the Sudan was better by 2000. This was partly because of the work of charities like Band Aid and Oxfam. Oxfam have helped the Sudanese to help themselves by supporting farming and small businesses, and by providing schools and clean water supplies. However, by 2000 there was a terrible famine in Ethiopia because of a drought there from 1997 to 2000. The famine meant that 10.5 million people were at risk of starvation. (*Source:* Oxfam UK 2002)	**Patriot Act, USA** The Patriot Act was passed in October 2001, after the terrorist attacks on America of 11 September. The Act said that people could be guilty of helping terrorism if they gave money to a group suspected of supporting the aims of groups suspected of plotting against the USA or American interests at home or abroad. The Act was added to in November when President Bush said that any non-American terrorist suspect could be tried by a military tribunal not a criminal court. This tribunal could hear the case in private, without lawyers, guilt could be decided by a two-thirds vote and without a jury. Anyone found guilty could be executed without any reason having to be given or any public statement.
Religion in China In China, freedom to worship does not exist and many religious groups are banned. For example, in 2001, 17 members of a Christian Church – the Huanan South China Church – were arrested. Twelve were given prison sentences of two years to life. Five were sentenced to death. There were also allegations of torture. China uses execution widely for many crimes, including tax fraud. It also tries to charge, try and execute many people very quickly. More people were executed in China between April and June 2001 than in the rest of the world from 1998 to 2001. (*Source:* Amnesty International 2002)	**Equal pay in United Kingdom** On Women's Day 2002 the Equal Opportunities Commission reported that female graduates were paid 15 per cent less than male graduates by the age of 24 years. The gap got wider as they got older. This was pay for female and male graduates who had studied the same subjects, got the same degree and were doing the same job. The Commission launched a campaign with the slogan 'Why are Women Graduates still going cheap?' to change employer attitudes. The Commission also reported that women doing management jobs were earning 24 per cent less each hour than male managers. (*Source:* Equal Opportunities Commission 2002)

Find out:

What did/do these people have to do with human rights?
Write a short bulletin – maximum 200 words – on three of them and their connection to human rights.

Eleanor Roosevelt	Nelson Mandela	Mahatma Gandhi
Arundhati Roy	Emmeline Pankhurst	Roger Caseman
Nye Bevan	Malcolm X	Bob Geldof
The Mothers of Plaza del Maya	Aung San Suu Kyi	

In Activity B, pupils could be shown an extract from the BBC programme *Newsround* and asked to make a script for *Newsround* about their chosen individuals.

Activity C: Why are there abuses of human rights? How can we stop them?

Target Group: Years 8 to 9

Learning Objectives
I should learn:

- Some of the reasons why rights get abused.
- To evaluate causes against evidence.
- How to take action ourselves to protect human rights.

Curriculum Links
History: Rights and abuses of rights. Using evidence to evaluate causes.
Art and Design: Design images to communicate ideas and beliefs about human rights.

Suggest the following as possible causes for abuses of human rights.

Fear	**Greed**	**Anger**	**Love**	**Ignorance**

Use Resource 6 'Do all people have their human rights?' to evaluate each possible cause. Which cause or causes do the pupils feel are important to understanding why there are abuses of human rights in the world?

For example, think about the content of the Patriot Act and why it was introduced (post 11 September 2001). How far does each of the above – fear, anger, greed, love, ignorance – help us to understand why the Patriot Act was introduced?

Care must be taken not to suggest that powerful feelings make an abuse of human rights legitimate.

Taking Community Action!
(i) Set up your own Student Amnesty International Group at school. Amnesty International publishes a pack to support such groups, has online resources, holds conferences and runs competitions especially for schools.
(ii) The slogan for Amnesty International is 'Writing Wrongs'. Start a campaign called 'Drawing Rights'. Choose one human rights' abuse and design a poster to raise awareness of it in your class/school/community.

Activity D: What happens when human rights conflict?

Target Group: Years 8 to 9

Learning Objectives
I should learn:

- That there are different interpretations of human rights – that is, different people have different ideas about 'what is a human right'.
- About some of the conflicts about human rights in the world today.
- The role of the United Nations and the European Court of Human Rights.

Curriculum Links
History: Rights and abuses of rights.
Religious Education: Nature of being human. Conflicting values and beliefs.

Different groups, such as 'pro abortion', 'pro Life', CND, anti-pornography, feminist, fascist, anti-fascist, have interpreted the Universal Declaration of Human Rights in different ways and used it to argue very different views.

Show the pupils the 'Human rights conflicts' below. They could be shared out between pupils or used by all the class together.

(i) Which articles of the Universal Declaration of Human Rights might each fit in with?
(ii) Which articles of the Universal Declaration of Human Rights might each conflict with?
(iii) How could these conflicts be solved?
(iv) Find out the role of the European Court of Human Rights in Strasbourg.
(v) Find out the role of the United Nations.

Human rights conflicts		
Right to abortion	*against*	Right to life
Right to freedom of speech		Right to respect/privacy
Right to arm for defence		Right to safety from all weapons of mass destruction, including nuclear

3 Law, Justice and Crime

About this chapter

This chapter is closely linked to and logically follows on from Chapter 2 on Human Rights. It begins by looking at the relationship between the law and rights and responsibilities. It then looks at the different parts and functions of the criminal justice system for adults and children. Pupils find out about the function of the different courts and legal personnel through role-play and research. Stories about miscarriages of justice are used to critically examine the challenges of justice as well as to understand the importance of the right of appeal.

1. What is a law? Who makes the law?

Activity A: What are rules and laws? Who makes them? Why?

Target Group: Year 8

Learning Objectives
I should learn:

- That laws in society are like rules at school.
- That laws protect rights.
- What the police and judges have to do with law.

Curriculum Links
History: Rights and responsibilities. Justice and law in the past, including the Middle Ages.

Refer back to Chapter 2, particularly Activity B, 'What are our rights and responsibilities at school?'. Use as a way of introducing school 'rules'. Discuss some school rules in depth. What is the point of the rule? How is it fair and just? How do school rules protect rights? In what ways are laws like school rules? Who decides rules at school?

Pupils write their own definitions of laws. Share them around the class through presentation, swapping, display. Use to agree a definition of a 'law'.

Ask pupils what parliament, judges and the police have to do with laws. Resource 7 shows the different roles. It could be cut up and pupils asked to put it together correctly.

There is an opportunity here to follow up with learning in history. For example, justice in the Middle Ages. How would justice have been done then? Combat (God will be on the side of the just and make them win), 'endurance tests' and the jury system are based on different ideas about people, gods, etc. What were these ideas? What changes occurred in crime and punishment over time?

Resource 7: Activity A: What are rules and laws? Who makes them? Why?

WHO MAKES LAWS? That is – decides what is a crime and what is not. ↓
PARLIAMENT
WHO DECIDES ABOUT GUILT, INNOCENCE, PUNISHMENT? That is – who decides how the laws should be used when a person is on trial? ↓ JUDGES MAGISTRATES JURIES
WHO ENFORCES LAWS? That is – decides who is breaking the law in the first place! ↓
POLICE

2. How can we get justice?

Activity A: How can we reach just and fair judgements?

Target Group: Year 8

Learning Objectives
I should learn:

- That there are different ways of solving conflict and getting justice.
- Why seeing the needs and rights of both 'sides' in a conflict is important.
- That talking and negotiating can be an important part of justice and fairness.

Curriculum Links
Drama: Using role play to investigate justice and how to resolve conflict.
History: Rights and responsibilities.

Refer back to learning on human rights (Chapter 2), particularly the purpose of school rules – to protect pupil and teacher rights at school. Ask what 'rules' are called in the wider community of Britain. Introduce the idea of British 'laws' as being there to protect rights of people in Britain.

Engage the pupils by introducing two characters from the same community. Two pupils could be asked to 'hot seat' as the two characters: Mr Brown and Mrs Scarlet. They live next door to each other. Mr Brown is sad because Mrs Scarlet has planted very fast growing evergreen trees along their boundary hedge. Now the trees are so tall he doesn't get any sun. Mrs Scarlet is angry that Mr Brown has asked her to cut them down. She has planted them because she doesn't like to be disturbed by Mr Brown's children playing in the garden.

Tell the pupils they are the 'judges' and will decide what should happen. Talk to the pupils about three possible 'solutions':

- Forcing Mrs Scarlet to cut down the trees.
- Telling Mr Brown to put up and shut up.
- Getting them together to agree on a solution.

Brainstorm possible agreements.

- Which agreements are responding to the *needs and rights* of both people?
- Why are these the best agreements?

Review the discussion, using it to stress the need in such negotiations to:

- Get both sides talking.
- Know what their different needs are.
- Get them to recognise each other's needs.

Tell the pupils that they will all now take part in a role play of similar situations.

Assessment opportunities
There are good opportunities in this activity to assess speaking and listening skills (see Appendix A) as well other assessment criteria that link to the learning objectives.

Resource 8: Activity A: How can we reach just and fair judgements?

Role Play: How can we get justice?

Groups A and B: 'The Disputants'

Share out the role play cards between 10 pupils.
Groups A and B are the ones who have 'a problem' or 'the disputants'.
They should help each other prepare their roles in two groups (A and B).

- Why are they angry with the 'other' side?
- What do they think is unfair?
- What are their needs and rights?

Group C: 'The Judges'

As equal members of this community, all the others must help the two sides reach an agreement that solves their conflict and that is just or fair. While Groups A and B are preparing, Group C studies the 'rules' and discusses their role as the 'judges'.

- In this community, there are no laws. All cases are judged individually.
- The community must talk until they reach an agreement that all accept.
- The talking should focus on finding a way to satisfy everyone's needs and rights.
- If they cannot agree, they must call in an outsider (the teacher) who will decide what is to be done.
- The judges will have to listen very carefully to each other and build on what each other are saying.

The role play.
Pupils with cards A1 and B1 either come to the front or sit in the middle of a circle.
They read out their cards.
The judges ask them questions and guide them to an agreement.
Repeat with cards A2 and B2, and so on.

Resource 8 (continued)

Card A1. You have four children aged 8 to 14. You live in a flat on Daisy Street. You have no garden. Your children like to play in the street and ride their bikes. You let them but only if they stay on the pavement. You want them to be allowed to do this.	**Card B1.** You are 70 years old. You live alone in a house on Daisy Street with a garden. You like to walk to the corner shop twice a day. You like children but you are worried about being knocked over by children on bikes. You want them to stop riding and playing on the pavement.
Card A2. You are a teenager who loves to draw, especially graffiti. You like to put colourful pictures and messages on walls. You live in the middle of town and there are lots of empty shops, subways and warehouses to draw on. You don't graffiti on people's houses. You want to carry on.	**Card B2.** You live in the centre of town. You have a lovely home and garden that you take great care of. But you hate graffiti on buildings. You don't see the point and think it spoils your community. Every time you see graffiti you feel angry. You want it to stop.
Card A3. You are a teenager whose parents have split up. Your mother wants you to stay with her but your father wants you to live with him. They live four miles apart. You wish you could stay with each of them. They are very angry with each other and not speaking.	**Card B3.** You are the father of a teenager. You have just split up with his/her mother and moved out of the family home. You miss your child and want him/her to come and live with you. You are very upset and angry. You do not want to speak to the mother.
Card A4. You are a 25 year old who was drinking and driving. You caused an accident and the person driving the other car was killed.	**Card B4.** You are the parent of a 22 year old who was killed by the person on Card A4 who caused a car accident because of drinking and driving.
Card A5. Five years ago you lent your friend £500. You did not sign anything but trusted them. They did not pay you back so one day, very angry, you went to their house and stole their TV. You think it is worth about £500.	**Card B5.** Five years ago your friend gave you £500. You do not think you should have to pay them back and you are very angry that they took your TV away.

Questions

What sort of problem does this system work best with?
What sort of problem does it work less well with?
In which cases would it have helped to have 'laws' to refer to/be guided by? All/some/none? Why? Why not?
Did you need to send anyone to prison? Why? Why not?

Activity B: How do we get justice in Britain today?

Target Group: Year 8

Learning Objectives
I should learn:

- How the criminal justice system works in Britain.
- What happens when an adult breaks the law.
- What happens when a juvenile (child) breaks the law.

Curriculum Links
Drama: Use of role play to explore the criminal justice system.

Refer back to Activity A: How can we reach just and fair judgements? How was the system of justice used different to the one in Britain today? How was it the same? Why might it be useful to have laws to guide judges?

Give pupils a copy of Resource 9.

Resource 9: Activity B: How do we get justice in Britain today?

What happens when someone breaks the law?

	Police Catch someone breaking the **law**. They **investigate** the crime. They question the person caught and any **witnesses**.	
	Police Decide whether the person can be charged with a crime or just warned or let off completely. If they think there is enough **evidence**, they pass case to:	
	Crown Prosecution Service (CPS) CPS decides whether or not to press charges depending on whether it thinks there are gounds for prosecution. They ask themselves two questions: Is there enough evidence? Is it in the interest of the public? If the answers are both 'yes', the	
	Police Press **charges**. They also decide if the person should be in jail or free while waiting to go on **trial**. They ask themselves two questions: Is the person dangerous? Will they run away? ↙ ↘	
If the answers are both 'No', the person goes out on **Bail**		If the answers are both 'Yes', the person goes to jail on **Remand**

Resource 9 (continued)

	CPS In the meantime the CPS prepares a case for trial at	
	Court ↙ There are two types: ↘	
Magistrates Court Magistrates Courts have no jury. Magistrates act as the judge. Magistrates only try less serious crimes, for example, theft, drunk and disorderly.		**Crown Court** Crown Courts have a **jury** and a judge. They try more serious crimes, for example, rape, murder, armed robbery. In the Crown Court, there are **prosecution lawyers** who try to prove the case and **defence lawyers** who try to defend the person.
	Guilty! If the defendant is found guilty, they are fined or sent to prison.	
	Prison Is used to: Punish Set an example to others Protect others Rehabilitate/make a person better	

Use dictionaries, textbooks and ICT to write a '**Legal Glossary**' of each of the words in bold in the sentences in Resource 9 (e.g. **law, investigate, witnesses**).

Use the Resources in this chapter, and information from the websites (listed under 'Chapter 3') in the Useful Contacts section at the back of the book, to find out:

What happens when children break the law?
What differences are there to an adult?

Use the cases in the role play referred to earlier (see Resource 8). For each case listed below, use the diagram (Resource 9) to discuss what would happen to the person in real life:

- The old person in B1 lost their temper and slapped one of the children on the face.
- The teenager in A2 has been caught doing graffiti by the police.
- The father in B3 has to go to court to try to get shared custody of his child.
- The driver in A4 has been charged with manslaughter.
- The person in A6 has asked the police to charge their friend with theft of the television.

The cases above could also be used to do one to five role plays of cases of law.

The organisations listed in the Useful Contacts section at the back of this book have information on how to role play a Magistrates Court; in particular the website of the Magistrates Association has specific information on how to organise a visit to a court.

Activity C: Why have some people failed to get justice?

Target Group: Years 8 to 9

Learning Objectives
I should learn:

- That the criminal justice system sometimes fails, and why.
- About the right of appeal and why it is important to have such a right.

Curriculum Links
History: Crime and punishment, law, justice and human rights.

Resource 10: Activity C: Why have some people failed to get justice?

Four stories about failures of justice

The Story of Stephen Lawrence

In 1993, a teenager called Stephen Lawrence was murdered in a racist attack. Nobody has ever been convicted of his murder. In 1999, a Report of an offical inquiry into his death was published. It was called the Macpherson Report after the leader of the inquiry. The Report concluded that justice had failed Stephen because of 'institutional racism' in the British criminal justice system. 'Institutional racism' means that racism was built into the police, law courts, prisons, etc. Racism formed part of the way some people thought, behaved and acted. Racism in the police, for example, meant that some of them did their job badly. They failed to give first aid to Stephen. The police involved refused to listen to eye witnesses who said it had been a racist attack. Assuming a fight between friends, they failed to follow up suspects, carry out house-to-house searches, keep notes of interviews and witness accounts. Some officers referred to Stephen, his friends and family as 'negro'.

The Story of the 'Guildford Four'

In October 1989 the Court of Appeal in Britain overturned the convictions of the 'Guildford Four'. The four, three men and one woman, had been found guilty in 1975 of planting bombs in Guildford and Woolwich in 1974, which killed seven people. The Court of Appeal found that the police had changed or made up some of the evidence. They also made public that, in 1979, a group of IRA members on trial for a different offence had admitted planting the bombs in Guildford and Woolwich. After the release of the Guildford Four, the Court of Appeal looked at another case. This case was called the 'Birmingham Six'. In 1974, 21 people were killed in pub bombings in Birmingham. Six Irishmen were found guilty of the murders. But in 1991 they also were released. It was found that torture had been used to get their 'confessions' and that the forensic evidence was unreliable. On release Gerry Conlon who served 15 years said: 'If there is a hell, it is being in prison and knowing you are innocent.'

The Story of Stephen Downing

In 1974, Stephen Downing, aged 17 (legally a child), was convicted of the murder of a woman who he found battered to death in a local cemetery. At the time, Stephen had some learning difficulties and the reading age of an 11 year old. His family and a local journalist campaigned for his release. After 27 years in prison he was finally released after an appeal court said his conviction was unsafe. There was evidence that the police ignored his rights during questioning – failing to tell him he was under arrest, failing to get him a lawyer, questioning him for seven hours, shaking him to keep him awake. Stephen Downing could have been released after 17 years – but he would have had to confess to the murder – something he always refused to do.

The Story of Sara Thornton

Sara Thornton murdered her husband in 1989 by stabbing him to death as he lay on the settee in a drunken sleep. She pleaded not guilty to murder but to manslaughter on the grounds of provocation – that her husband regularly beat her. This plea was not accepted and the following year she was jailed for life at Birmingham Crown Court.

Under pressure from women's groups, her case was referred back to the Court of Appeal and a retrial was ordered. Thornton's supporters said that she was a battered wife pushed to desperate measures by a drunken, bullying husband. In May 1996, Thornton was convicted of manslaughter on unspecified grounds. She was sentenced to five years' imprisonment, time she had already served.

Resource 10 (continued)

Questions

Discuss each case in turn:
How helpful are the following in understanding why justice doesn't always work?

Prejudice	Ignorance	Pressure on police	Racism	Sexism	Fear	Poverty

Why is it important to have a 'right of appeal'?

4 Power, Democracy and Politics

About this chapter

This chapter begins by introducing ideas about power, its nature and function, through an extended role play of an imaginary community of teenagers. Pupils learn to correctly use terms such as democratic, fair, just, equal. They learn how power is shared within real political systems and about the history of the struggle for the franchise in the nineteenth and twentieth centuries. Pupils find out about the function of voting in democracies, about increasing political apathy and reflect on its causes. They discuss the challenges facing minorities within democracies. They find out why some groups oppose the first past the post voting system in the UK in favour of alternatives. Lastly, they find out how government works, including the function of the Cabinet.

1. Who has power?

Activity A: Thinking about power and government

Target Group: Year 7

Learning Objectives
I should learn:

- To use terms such as power, ruler, govern, role, responsibility.
- To think about power and government in relation to school.

Curriculum Links
History: Links with study of government, kingship, power.

Draw on pupils' knowledge and understanding of roles and responsibilities at school to introduce discussion of 'rulers', 'government', 'councils', etc. Brainstorm all words to do with rule and government, for example, governors, head, power, laws.

At school
Who is in charge? One person/group?
Do people have different roles? What? Why?

School Council
Does the school have a School Council?
What powers does it have?
What is its role? Responsibilities?
How are representatives chosen?
Are they representative of the school population?
Think about sex, age, ethnicity, etc.

Activity B: Why do people obey rulers?

Target Group: Year 7

Learning Objectives
I should learn:

- That in the past and today people have obeyed and obey rulers and governments for different reasons.

Curriculum Links
History: At Key Stages 2 and 3 pupils will have found out about different systems of government.

Which rulers have they studied in history lessons? How did they get their power? By the sword? By religion? By voting? By birth? How is that different to Britain today? Depending which periods of time the pupils have studied, match their knowledge of different rulers to the people shown in Resource 11.

Resource 11: Activity B: Why do people obey rulers?

Why obey rulers?

2. About different political systems

Activity A: The Island

Target Group: Years 8 to 9

Learning Objectives
I should learn:

- About different ways of ruling a community.
- The challenges of fair government/rule.
- To think about and make judgements about different systems.
- To take part in a role play, making decisions and reflecting on those decisions.

Curriculum Links
Geography: Settlements, Maps, Land Features, Food, Farming, Resources, Water.
History: Different political systems in the past. Rights and power – Magna Carta and King John.
English Literature: Novels such as *Coral Island, Lord of the Flies, Animal Farm.*
Literacy: Language of persuasion.

This activity could take several sessions, depending on how it is presented to the pupils. A link can be made to a similar exercise, 'Our Worlds', about political systems and human rights (see Chapter 2, Activity A: Making rules for our world, p. 31).

Resource 12: Activity A: The Island

Part 1

About 60 of you have been shipwrecked and marooned on an island in the middle of the sea. All the adults are dead. You must look after yourselves while you wait for a ship to come along. You have some vegetable seeds with you, some bottles, an axe, a bucket, a First Aid Kit, chalk, but nothing else.

The island looks like this:

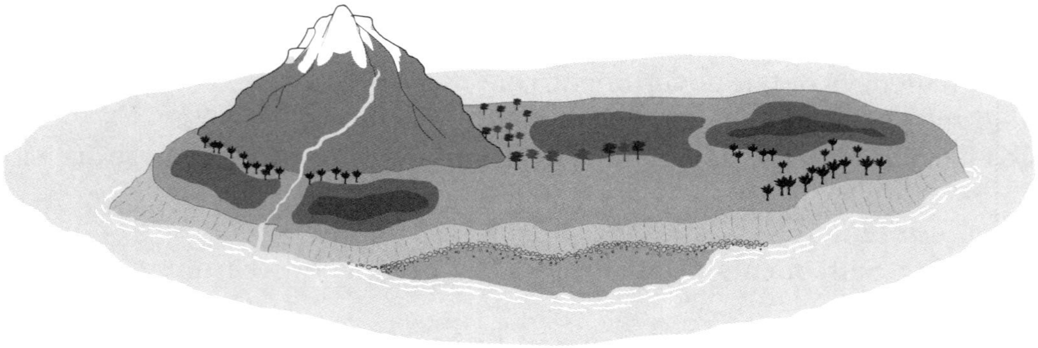

In order to stay alive, you must make decisions about:

Food

How will you eat?
Who will catch fish?
Who will pick fruit?
Who will plant vegetables?

Water

Who will fetch water from the mountain stream to the settlement?

Shelter

What will you use to build houses?
Who will build them?

But first you must discuss:

(i) Who will be the ruler/rulers?
(ii) What powers will they have?

Who will make all the decisions? Who will be 'in charge'? What will the 'rules' be? Who will make the rules?
Will it be:

- One ruler
- Small group of rulers
- Everyone
- Other

Resource 12 (continued)

In making your decisions, you should think about:
How will the ruler(s) be chosen? Will he/she/they be elected? Will there be volunteers for ruler(s)? Will those who want to rule fight it out? Will it be the same person/group all the time or will everyone take it in turns? For how long? Will the ruler(s) do other work or will they rule all the time? How much power will they have over everyone else? If power is to be given to one person/group, will everyone else be able to check that they are doing a good job? How? How can the ruler(s) be changed if need be? Who will decide this?

Questions

Think about your system:
What are its strong points?
What are its weak points?
What new problems might your Island community face over time, e.g. six months?

Resource 12 (continued)

Part B

You have been on the Island for six months and there is no sign of rescue.
There are new problems to solve:

- Some people are bored.
- Some people are stealing and fighting.
- Some people are sick or injured and need caring for.
- Everyone is not doing his or her fair share.

Discuss how you could solve these problems.
As a class, brainstorm and discuss what you have learnt about:

(a) Power
(b) Government

Activity B: Who rules in the real world? How?

Target Group: Years 8 to 9

Learning Objectives
I should learn:

- Differences between democracy, dictatorship and royalty.
- To think about and make judgements about different systems.

Curriculum Links
History: In history pupils learn about different forms of government throughout the Programme of Study.

Hand out Resource 13 'Who rules in the real world? How?'. Pupils match type of system to description.

Use sources of information (history textbooks, ICT, newspapers, political maps) to work out which type of political system listed in Resource 13 exists in the countries listed below, or to which the country's system is most similar:

India	Britain	South Africa
Burma	Cuba	Russia
China	Israel	Chile
France	Iraq	Uzbekistan
USA	Saudi Arabia	

Some countries may have a combination of more than one; for example, a dictator elected by voting.

Pupils use Part 2 of Resource 13 to evaluate the strong and weak points of each system. They will need to look at them from the point of view of rulers and ruled. For example, dictatorships are often found in countries recovering from colonial rule or war because they can be very stable systems. Democracies depend, in part, on literate populations with good communication systems.

Resource 13: Activity B: Who rules in the real world? How?

Political systems

Read the following descriptions of real life political systems and:
(a) Match the description to the correct type of system.
(b) Which is the most similar to your Island?

Types of system:

- Royalty/Kingship
- Democracy
- Dictatorship

Part 1

Description	**Type**
Ruled by one person with a government who do what he/she says. There is no voting or elections. No opposition groups are allowed. People cannot criticise the ruler. If they do they are put in prison or executed. The army is also important and often used to support rule.	
All rulers have been elected by the people to represent them. There are elections every five years. Everyone over 18 years can vote. Freedom of speech is protected. Opposition groups are allowed. The rulers can be questioned about how they are ruling.	
The ruler is the King or Queen. They are the ruler because they were born into the royal family. They are helped by a government. Many of the important jobs in the government are held by members of the royal family.	

Resource 13 (continued)

Part 2

Dictatorship
Strong points: **Weak points:**
Democracy **Strong points:**   **Weak points:**
Royalty **Strong points:**   **Weak points:**

3. All about voting and democracy

Activity A: Who had to fight to get the vote? Why?

Target Group: Years 8 to 9

Learning Objectives
I should learn:

- About different people, power and government in the past.
- Why some men and all women had to fight for the vote.
- When changes happened in the franchise in Britain.
- When women got the vote across Europe.
- About the different roles of men and women in the nineteenth and early twentieth century and how they changed.

Key words
Franchise OR The right to vote in elections to choose Members of Parliament (MPs)
Suffrage

Curriculum Links
History: At Key Stage 3 pupils study industrialisation and political reform.
Art: Portrait painting and gender. The National Portrait Gallery has a very good website where portraits can be viewed and analysed. What messages do they send? Many portraits from the nineteenth century raise issues about sex and gender, men, women, power.

Has everyone always been able to vote?
Refer to School Council voting or call a vote on an important and topical issue in the class. Exclude one group (e.g. left handers, blond hair, boys). Discuss how it feels to be excluded.

Teachers could also use or link to Activity A: 'Making rules for our world' on human rights in Chapter 2 (p. 31).

Establish that in the past not everyone could vote and that this was based on ideas people had about:

- What sort of people were fit to vote.
- What women were like – their feelings, behaviour, strengths, weaknesses.
- What men were like.
- What the poor were good at.
- What the rich were good at.

When did the franchise change?
Give pupils copies of Resource 14 'Timeline of changes in franchise 1815 to 1928' or display on OHT.

Discuss what it shows about ideas about power, men, women and property.

Test pupils' understanding by asking them to work out the date when each of the following characters would have got the vote:

- Working-class woman aged 23 working in a factory in Lancashire.
- Rich farmer in Sussex. He owns forests, land, cottages.
- Shopkeeper in Liverpool. He and his family live above the shop.
- Tenant farmer in Devon. Rents his house and fields from a big landowner.
- 42 year old woman married to a rich landowner in Kent.
- Rich merchant from Bristol. He owns a shipping company and warehouse.

What ideas did people have about who was fit to vote?
Study the sources of information in Resource 14 about property, about men and about women. What can you learn about ideas about voting and men and women?

Discuss with pupils how ideas about property, about men and about women help to explain why the franchise changed when it did *and* why it didn't change.

Test pupils' understanding by asking them to hot seat as the characters listed above. Question them about why they do not have the vote. How can they use what they know about ideas in the nineteenth century to explain why they could not vote?

Why did men and women want the vote?
Why did men and women want the vote? Brainstorm why it is important to be able to vote.

Resource 14: Activity A: Who had to fight to get the vote? Why?

Timeline of changes in franchise 1815 to 1928

1815	Very few men and no women could vote! The men who could vote were all rich. Most owned a lot of land. A few made their money in other ways such as merchants and bankers.	13 per cent of adult men. No women.
1832	**Great Reform Act** changed the law about voting. It said that every male householder (man with a house) worth a certain amount could vote. But it only changed the vote in the towns. Most middle-class men in towns could vote after 1832.	18 per cent of adult men. No women.
1867	**Second Reform Act** changed the law again about voting. All male householders in the towns could vote. Many of these were working-class men. More male householders were given the vote in the countryside too. In the towns and cities, working-class men were now the biggest group of voters.	36 per cent of adult men. No women.
1884	**Third Reform Act** changed the law again about voting. This was needed because after 1867 there was still a big difference between the towns and the countryside regarding who could vote. This Act gave the vote to all male householders in the countryside as well as the towns.	65 per cent of adult men. No women.
1918	**Franchise Act** let women vote for the first time. It gave the vote to women over 30 who were householders or wives of householders or who paid a rent of £5+. All men over 21 got the vote.	100 per cent of adult men (over 21). Women over 30 years old.
1928	**Equal Franchise Act** gave equal rights to vote to men and women for the first time. All men and women over 21 could now vote.	100 per cent of adult men and adult women (over 21).

Resource 14 (continued)

Ideas about property, men and women

A At the beginning of the nineteenth century many people believed that only landed gentry could vote. This was because people believed only they had the education and experience needed to make important decisions and be responsible for others. And as for women! Most people never even thought about women voting at this time. *(An historian in the twenty-first century)*
B By the mid nineteenth century many things had changed and carried on changing into the late nineteenth century. There had been revolutions on the European continent where working classes had rebelled and taken power from their rulers. Many British politicians thought it was better to give some of the working class the vote to stop revolution.
C There were certain things which women could do better than men, and others which they could not do as well. In all that required rough, rude, practical force, stability of character, and intellect, man was superior: whereas in all those relations of life that demanded mildness, softness of character and amiability, women far excelled. *(An MP in a debate in Parliament about whether women should get vote in 1867)*
D At the end of the nineteenth and in the early twentieth century suffragettes (prepared to use violent, militant methods) and suffragists (non-violent) campaigned for the vote for women. The First World War showed that women could be leaders, managers, organisers, decision makers and were capable of wielding power and taking responsibility.

Resource 14 (continued)

Why did men and women want the vote?

The extracts below all help us to understand why people wanted to be able to vote.

Women and marriage

In the early and mid nineteenth century, women had very few rights in marriage. Married women were under the control of their husbands. They could not own their own property. They could not move out and go and live in another house. They could not divorce husbands for being violent, only unfaithful. If there was a divorce, mothers could not have custody of their children. Some people, such as Caroline Norton, Mary Wollstonecraft, John Stuart Mill, wanted to change the laws but they could not. They could not change the law because they had very little support in parliament.
History Textbook, 2001

Corn Laws 1815

These laws were hated by many in the towns and the poor in the countryside because they made bread very expensive. The farmers liked the laws because they helped farmers. The laws stopped foreign imports of food, including wheat. This made prices of bread in Britain more expensive because there was less wheat to go around and less competition from others. Many poor people and town people wanted to change the laws but they could not. They could not change the law because they could not vote.
History Textbook, 2001

Poverty among the working class

Our husbands are overworked, our houses ill-furnished, our families ill-fed, and our children uneducated. The fear of want hangs over our heads. . . . We are powerless because we are poor.
Anne Knight, Chartist in Northern Star newspaper, 1849

Contagious Diseases Acts 1866 and 1869

In Victorian times, sexually transmitted diseases like syphilis and gonorrhoea were big killers. Women prostitutes were often blamed for spreading the diseases, and for being prostitutes. Men were not often blamed. The Acts said that women suspected of being prostitutes could be forced to have a medical examination. Men could not be forced. This was unfair and meant the disease was not stopped. People, especially women, like Josephine Butler, wanted the law changed but women did not have the vote. This meant they had no power over the MPs who made the law. They could not change the law because they could not vote.
History Textbook, 2001

Militant suffragettes

We never went to prison in order to be martyrs. We went there in order that we might obtain the rights of citizenship. We were willing to break laws that we might force men to give us the right to make laws.
Emmeline Pankhurst, Suffragette leader 1920s

National Union of Women's Suffrage Societies

Because as long as women cannot vote . . . they are treated like children who do not know what is good or bad for them.

Because laws are made which specifically affect women's work and the work of their children.

Because the way to help women is to give them the means of helping themselves.

From pamphlet called 'Some Reasons Why Working Women Want the Vote' by NUWSS, 1913

Stress that many different and courageous individuals and groups fought for the vote. Some died for it.

As individuals, in pairs, or in groups, pupils research these questions:

- When did they live?
- What were their ideas about voting?
- About women? About men and property?
- Did they belong to a group? If yes, which one?
- What action did they take?
- What were their achievements?

About these people:

- John Locke
- Edmund Burke
- Mary Wollstonecraft
- Harriet Taylor
- Josephine Butler
- John Stuart Mill
- Pankhursts – Emmeline, Christabel and Sylvia
- Millicent Fawcett

They must write a Short Biography for an encyclopaedia of 'Famous People and The Vote'. No more than 300 words about each person.

Resource 14 (continued)

When did women get the vote across Europe?

Dates female suffrage achieved across Europe			
Finland	1906	Spain	1931
*Portugal	1910	Turkey	1934
Norway	1913	France	1944
Denmark	1915	Bulgaria	1944
Iceland	1915	Hungary	1945
Poland	1918	Albania	1945
The former Soviet Union	1918	Italy	1945
Austria	1918	Romania	1946
Germany	1918	Malta	1947
Ireland	1918	Belgium	1948
Netherlands	1919	The former Yugoslavia	1949
Luxembourg	1919	Greece	1952
The former Czechoslovakia	1920	Cyprus	1960
Sweden	1921	Monaco	1962
UK	1928	Switzerland	1971

The above Table can be used with other sources of information, including maps and timelines, to investigate European trends and triggers in relation to women's suffrage. Use the Table to investigate:

- patterns – geographical patterns and patterns relating to political, religious and other differences and possible exceptions to patterns (Turkey? France? Belgium? Switzerland?);
- relationship of suffrage to other events, e.g. war, political change;
- impact of the cultural context, including religious beliefs.

* Women in Portugal got the vote in 1910, but their citizenship and democratic rights could not always be exercised under the rule of Salazar from 1926 to 1974.

4. How democratic is Britain?

Activity A: What is voter apathy?

Target Group: Year 9

Learning Objectives
I should learn:

- How voter 'turnout' has changed since 1945.
- What is 'voter apathy' and some of its causes.
- About different kinds of voting systems, their advantages and disadvantages.
- Differences between 'First Past the Post', 'Proportional Representation', 'Additional Member System'.
- To use numeracy skills to analyse political issues.

Curriculum Links
History: Democracy, representative democracy, voting systems.
Languages: Comparisons of voter turnout in European countries. The website of the Electoral Reform Society includes statistics.
Numeracy: Application of number, including use of percentages and statistics.

Display Resource 15 Tables 1 and 2 on an OHT or hand out to pupils.
Discuss what it shows. Talk about the two main voting systems: First Past the Post and Proportional Representation. Do a quick First Past the Post vote in class. Get pupils to reach a definition of the term. Use Table 2 to explain and discuss 'Proportional Representation'.

Questions
- Study Table 1
  - 1.(i) What do you notice about changes in voter turnout between 1945 and 2001?
  - (ii) Write one sentence to describe the most important change.
  - 2. What do you think is meant by 'voter apathy'?
  - 3. Why might people be worried about it?
  - 4. Why do you think 1945 is lower than 1950?
- Study Table 2
  1. What percentage of the vote did the Liberal Democrat party win in 2002?
  2. What percentage of seats in parliament did the Liberal Democrat party win in 2002?
  3. What percentage of the vote did the Labour party win in 2002?
  4. What percentage of seats in parliament did the Labour party win in 2002?
  5. What is unfair about this?
  6. How could 'Proportional Representation' help the Liberal Democrats?
  7. Could 'Proportional Representation' make the UK more democratic? Why? Why not?

- Study Tables 1 and 2
  1. Use the information in both Tables to work out approximately what percentage of the adult population voted for the Labour party in 2002.

Note: Membership of political parties has also gone down. However, more people are joining other types of organisations, e.g. RSPCA, RSPB, Greenpeace, Friends of the Earth, etc.

Resource 15: Activity A: What is voter apathy?

Table 1: UK General Elections: electorates and turnout 1945–2001

Year	Electorate	Turnouts %*
1945	33,240,391	72.8
1950	34,412,255	83.9
1951	34,919,331	82.6
1955	34,852,179	76.8
1959	35,397,304	78.7
1964	35,894,054	77.1
1966	35,957,245	75.8
1970	39,342,013	72.0
February 1974	39,753,863	78.8
October 1974	40,072,970	72.8
1979	41,095,649	76.0
1983	42,192,999	72.7
1987	43,180,753	75.3
1992	43,249,721	77.7
1997	43,765,391	71.5
2001	44,405,826	59.4

*Total valid vote as a percentage of the electorate

Resource 15 (continued)

Table 2: Results of 2002 General Election

Party	Votes	% Votes	Seats	% Seats
Labour	10,724,895	40.7	412	62.5
Conservative	8,357,622	31.7	166	25.2
Liberal Democrats	4,812,833	18.3	52	7.9
SNP	464,305	1.8	5	0.8
Plaid Cymru	195,892	0.7	4	0.6
UKIP	390,575	1.5	–	–
Green	166,487	0.6	–	–
Scottish Socialist Party	72,279	0.3	–	–
Socialist Alliance	60,496	0.2	–	–
SLP	57,536	0.2	–	–
Northern Ireland parties	810,374	3.1	18	2.7
Others	255,504	0.9	2	0.3
Totals	26,368,798	100	659	100

(*Source:* Electoral Reform Society, 22 March 2002)

What are the arguments for change?

Discuss the common objections referred to in Resource 16 to the First Past the Post voting system used in the UK to elect parliament.

Resource 16: Activity A: What is voter apathy?

How democratic is Britain?

Activity B: Is voting enough?

Target Group: Years 8 to 9

Learning Objectives
I should learn:

- Why some minorities have problems getting a share of power in the UK.
- Why some minorities used and still use direct action and militancy to get attention.
- About different ways of campaigning for change.

Curriculum Links
History: Rights of minorities. Challenges of representative democracies.

This activity looks at the challenges facing minorities within democracies like the UK. These minorities face particular challenges *because* they are minorities. The first past the post system makes it harder for them to have a share of power.

A quick vote could be taken in the classroom to demonstrate the point. Choose a topic where there will be a minority. For example 'all people must write with right hand'. How could the left handers change this rule? Could they do it through voting?

Refer back to the suffragettes:

- Use history textbooks to establish that some supporters of votes for women used violence to try and get the vote. Some were willing to be sent to prison and go on hunger strike, be force-fed, to try and get change. Some died for the cause.

Discuss with pupils:

- Why did some suffragettes use violence to change laws about voting?
- What is the problem with trying to change a law if you don't have the vote?
- What is the problem with trying to change a law today if you are a minority?

Brainstorm all the minorities that pupils can think of:

- What problems might they face trying to change laws in the UK?
- Research in groups one of these minorities. What methods do they use to get change? Minorities include:
    Animal Rights supporters
    Disabled and impaired people
    Republican Catholics in Northern Ireland
    Pro-life, anti-abortionists
    Greenpeace
    Friends of the Earth

5. Government in the United Kingdom

Activity A: About British government

Target Group: Year 9

Learning Objectives
I should learn:

- Different roles and responsibilities of local and central government.
- How government works in the UK.
- Why Wales, Scotland and Ireland have their own governments.
- About the Welsh Assembly, Irish Assembly and Scottish Parliament.

Curriculum Links
History: Government in the UK. The making of the UK and devolution.
Geography: Different constituencies, including the UK, Britain.

Resource 17: Activity A: About British government

In England all of the tasks listed below are done either by the local council (borough, county, district, parish) or by central government (parliament). Sort them out into two columns.

Organising rubbish collection
Looking after street lighting
Making laws on crime
Repairing roads
Building swimming pools
Going to war against another country
Collecting taxes
Deciding pay for teachers
Organising the fire brigade
Deciding how many libraries to have
Deciding how much to spend on the army
Planning where to build new local authority housing
Planning where phone companies can put mobile phone masts
Deciding a law that controls the number of mobile phone masts

Questions

(a) What do you notice about the differences between the two columns?
(b) Write one or two sentences that explain why some things are done by the local council and some by central government. You could start like this:
Local government looks after things that
While central government looks after things that

Resource 18: Activity A: About British government

How government works in the UK

HOW GOVERNMENT WORKS

PEOPLE

Vote in General Elections for MPs to represent them in parliament
+
Vote in local elections for councillors to represent them on Councils (county/district/borough/unitary)

PARLIAMENT

Function:
(a) Makes laws
(b) Debates what government is doing about national and world affairs

COUNCILS

Function:
(a) Make decisions on local issues, e.g. roads, schools, leisure
(b) Debates local affairs and what council is doing

Made up of two 'Houses'

LORDS

Non-elected
Can be a Lord:
(i) by birth
(ii) by Church of England
(iii) nominated by main political parties

COMMONS

Elected MPs
(all MPs are elected)
Political party with the most MPs makes a GOVERNMENT

MINSTERS
SECRETARIES OF STATE
are chosen by Prime Minister to run government departments, e.g. Education

+

PRIME MINISTER
Leader of the government

CABINET
Made up of Prime Minister and other important ministers
Makes important decisions about policy which can then be debated in parliament

Resource 18 (continued)

Questions

Pupils make their own 'Guide to Government in the UK' for an audience of Year 8 pupils.
Copy the diagram and illustrate it for the guide.
Find out the meaning of all the words in italics and write your own glossary for the guide.

Note that Scotland, Wales and Northern Ireland have an extra 'layer' of government than England. This layer of government gets its power from the UK parliament. It has power to make decisions about national (Welsh, Scottish, Irish) matters.

In 1997 the Scots and the Welsh voted for 'devolution'. Devolution meant having some power devolved from central government in England to governments in Scotland and Wales. These new governments are called the Scottish Parliament and the Welsh Assembly. In 1998 the people of Northern Ireland voted for devolution too and the Northern Ireland Assembly was set up.

About the Welsh Assembly

The main task of the Welsh Assembly is to develop policies that reflect the particular needs of the people of Wales. Some Welsh people wanted an assembly because of the differences between England and Wales. Wales has a population of 4.9 million and nearly 25 per cent speak Welsh. This number is increasing because the National Curriculum in Wales requires children to learn Welsh at school. Although Wales does have manufacturing industries and some coal and steel industries left, many Welsh people live in rural areas. While the environment and quality of life is very good for many Welsh people, as a whole they tend to be poorer than other UK residents. On average, Welsh people in 2002 earned 80 per cent Gross Domestic Product (GDP) per head of the GDP of people living elsewhere in the UK.

The Welsh Assembly has power over and responsibility for agriculture, environment, education, culture and heritage, tourism, sport and leisure, industry, the Welsh language, health, town and country planning. However, it has no control over taxation, interest rates, laws, employment policies, social security policies and foreign affairs. These areas are decided in the UK Parliament in London and MPs from Welsh constituencies continue to have seats in the UK Parliament.

Ioan is a 14 year old boy who lives in Carmarthen. Ioan's parents were born in Wales but do not speak Welsh. Ioan speaks English at home and Welsh at school. He learnt Welsh at primary school and now he goes to a secondary Welsh-speaking school. Most of his lessons are in Welsh and in two years he will do all his GCSEs in Welsh. After school he sometimes watches children's TV – on Welsh and English channels. His local MP is in the Welsh Nationalist (Plaid Cymru) Party. He is a member of the UK parliament and of the Welsh Assembly.

Ioan has been finding out about British Government at school. He thinks that the Welsh Assembly is a good idea and he wants Wales to carry on being part of the UK.
What reasons might he have given for his political beliefs?

Questions

In the referendum for a Welsh Assembly, less than 50 per cent of the population voted in favour of having devolution. Imagine you are in the cabinet of the Welsh Assembly. Brainstorm answers to the questions:

What could be done to increase participation in and support for the Welsh Assembly?
Why is it important to do so?
Does England need an Assembly too? Why? Why not?

Activity B: How is Britain governed? The Cabinet

Target Group: Years 8 to 9

Learning Objectives
I should learn:

- That income from taxes is used for spending on the country's needs.
- How the government makes decisions and how the Cabinet works.
- About finance (money) and government.
- To reflect on what I have learnt in a role play.

Curriculum Links
History: Characteristics of government across time and place.
Numeracy: Application of number.
Literacy: Use of persuasive language.
Drama: Use of role play to investigate how the Cabinet works.

Refer pupils back to their guides 'How government works in the UK'. Ask pupils about the Prime Minister, Cabinet and ministers. Remind each other what their roles are.

The class will do the role play divided into two groups of up to 14, role playing as two Cabinets. However, the number of roles can be varied easily by excluding some ministers or adding some ministers.

Hand out the role cards to pupils. You may wish to think about pupils able to be Prime Minister (good communication and managing meeting skills) and the Chancellor of the Exchequer (good numeracy skills).

Give pupils about 10 minutes to prepare the role in 'same role groups'. For example, two Home Office ministers together, two Education ministers together and so on. Prime Ministers and Chancellors of the Exchequer should prepare in a group of four.

The length of the role play can vary. Pupils can do several stages over a series of lessons or a shorter version within one session. If over several lessons, encourage pupils to discuss it and plan their strategy in between. Pupils in role as ministers could be encouraged to form alliances with other ministers!
Stages might include:

(i) First discussion. All ministers state their aims and the money needed to achieve them. Priorities are discussed. PM responds with his views.
(ii) Second discussion. Chancellor presents some ideas. Discuss money further.
(iii) Third discussion. Agree priorities. Vote on policy.
(iv) Fourth discussion. Vote on policy and funding. PM gives final view.

The activity can be extended by pupils doing research either before or after the role play on the 'real' manifestos and the 'real' departments. All political parties and departments have websites (see the Useful Contacts section at the back of this book).

Resource 19: Activity A: 'How is Britain governed? The Cabinet

The Cabinet meeting
Instructions

You are going to role play a Cabinet meeting in the United Kingdom. Your party has just won the General Election and formed a government. It is your first time in government and you all want to do a very good job. You want to do good things for the people of the UK as well as keeping your party popular. You also have made lots of promises in your Manifesto before the election. Each Minister has a department to take charge of and three aims (see the role play cards). In this Cabinet meeting you all must decide your policy for the next 12 months and how to spend the £4 billion of money you have in your budget.

Prime Minister

Your job is to lead and manage the Cabinet meeting. You decide who speaks. You must listen to everyone. Ask questions. At the end of the discussion, you must ask for a vote to help you decide your priorities. But if there is a tie, the final word is yours!

Chancellor of the Exchequer

You are in charge of finance. You must also support the Prime Minister in leading the meeting. You will have to take lots of notes about money and make quick sums in your head. You must spend as much of your budget as possible but not a penny over. You must also look out for any extra sources of revenue (money coming in).

Ministers

Your job is to persuade the Prime Minister and Chancellor of the Exchequer that:

(a) Your department's aims are very important.
(b) Your aims should be a high priority for the government.
(c) Money from the budget should be given for your work to be done.

To prepare:

- Read the role card.

Think about:

- Which of your department's aims link to the manifesto? These are useful points to make because they show your government is fulfilling its promises!
- How might your aims help the country?
- How might your aims help the government stay popular?
- Do your aims help any other department? If so, this could be a good argument to use to gain allies!
- What other arguments could you use?
- How could you use your learning from science, history, geography, design, etc.?

During the discussion you must all take notes. How much do other people want? What are their arguments? How could you argue against them?

Resource 19 (continued)

The Manifesto

If we win power we promise to:

- Make the UK safer
- Improve public transport
- Make the UK a tourist attraction
- Raise the importance of the UK in the world
- Cut crime
- Raise standards in education
- Cut pollution and global warming
- Make people healthier

Questions

Compare your decisions to the other two Cabinets.
What was the same and what was different?
What difference might it have made to have a General Election coming in six months?

Take Community Action!

Visit the local Council office and watch a Council meeting.
Find out whether the local council uses 'Cabinets' or not. Different authorities have different systems.
How does your council make decisions?
Who has power?
Is power shared between different political parties?

Resource 19 (continued)

The Cabinet meeting
Role play cards

Prime Minister	Chancellor of the Exchequer
You are the leader of your party and the government. You can ask the Chancellor for help. But in the end, you decide what happens! You must listen carefully to all your Ministers. You must manage the meeting so that everyone speaks. You can call a vote on some issues if you want to.	Your job is very important. You manage all the finance for this government. The country must not go bankrupt! You collect money from taxes to spend on needs. You must help the Prime Minister decide how this year's budget must be spent. You have £4 billion (1,000 × million) to spend.
Minister of Home Office You are in charge of the Home Office, which includes crime, justice, immigration. Your aims are to: (i) **cut street crime.** It has risen dramatically recently. You need more police officers and youth clubs. Police officers will cost about £200 million, youth clubs about £150 million. (ii) **tackle the big problem of over crowding in prisons.** You need about £400 million to build new prisons. (iii) **take proper care of immigration.** You need more centres, more support, quicker legal processes. You need at least £300 million.	**Minister of Education** Your job is to raise standards. Everyone is very worried that British schools are getting worse. Your aims are to: (i) **do something about boys.** Most boys are not doing as well as girls at school. You need about £20 million for projects. (ii) **consider repairs. Many schools urgently need money for repairs.** It will cost about £300 million to repair them all. (iii) **consider salaries. Teachers want more pay.** They say they will strike without it. They haven't had a pay rise for six years. You need about £25 million to give them what they want.
Minister of Transport Your job is to improve transport without increasing pollution. Your aims are to: (i) **make more trains and buses and make them more punctual.** There have been many complaints. You need at least £300 million. (ii) **improve the roads.** There are terrible queues, especially in big cities and on motorways. You could charge tolls to make money; or build more roads at a cost of £150 million. (iii) **deal with a tree house anti-road demonstration in a wood around Newplace.** The last government said a bypass could be built there. The cost of policing the demonstration might be £2 million.	**Minister of Environment, Agriculture & Countryside** Your job is to take care of farming, the environment and the countryside. One of your big worries is tourism. A report shows fewer people are using the UK for holidays. Your aims are to: (i) **cut down on pollution in the UK, especially in cities.** You will need to have improved transport and rules on industrial pollution to do this. (ii) **get more tourists into the countryside and the cities.** You need £20 million for adverts and £150 million for tourist spots. (iii) **deal with the big problem of animal transport to France by lorry.** Animal rights supporters are campaigning that such transport is cruel. You might need to compensate farmers £50 million to stop it.

Resource 19 (continued)

Minister of Health

Your job is to take care of hospitals, nurses, doctors, and promote preventative health care, for example stop smoking adverts. A report has just come out which shows that alcohol costs the UK about £1 billion per year. Your aims are to:

(i) **cut long hospital waiting lists.** You will need about £500 million to do them all.
(ii) **GPs want a pay rise.** They had one three years ago. It would cost £100 million.
(iii) **deal with alcohol abuse.** You may need to ban alcohol adverts. This would lose revenue/income in taxes of £800 million.

Minister of Defence

Your job is to manage the armed forces (Army, Navy, Air Force), buy and sell arms (weapons) and defend the UK and, sometimes, its allies. Your aims are to:

(i) **decide how many soldiers, if any, should be sent to the war of an ally of the UK.** Sending soldiers could cost up to £80 million.
(ii) **decide whether to take part in the star wars defence system of the USA.** It will cost £600 million to take part.
(iii) **decide whether or not to sell weapons to a poor country in Asia that has a civil war**. It could make revenue of £50 million for the UK.

Minister of Culture, Media & Sport

Your job is to take care of entertainment (film, theatre, television), art and artefacts (museums, galleries), all sports and media (radio, newspapers, Internet). Your department has been ignored in the past and you are determined to make it a priority (more important). Your aims are to:

(i) **stop museums charging money.** Because of charges less people are going to museums and the poor cannot. Also tourists are upset about the charges. Cost will be about £60 million.
(ii) **donate £20 million to support British film making.**
(iii) **make a bid for the Olympics to be held in the UK.** It would be a big boost for the UK. You need at least £30 million to make the bid.

Minister of International Affairs

Your job is to take care of world concerns like disasters, poverty, war. Your department has been ignored in the past and you are determined to make it a priority (more important). You are against money being spent on weapons here and overseas. Your aims are to:

(i) **give £30 million to a disaster appeal after an earthquake in southern Italy.** They need new homes, food, water, medicines.
(ii) **support a vaccination programme in the horn of Africa.** The cost will be £30 million. It will save many children dying from diseases.
(iii) **support a psychological schools service for Balkan children upset by the wars in their countries.** It will cost £15 million to employ psychologists and pay for teacher training.

Minister for Wales

Your job is to protect Welsh interests. At the moment money is needed for Welsh films. Also there are fewer hospitals in Wales than England. This means Welsh people have to travel further to hospital. Your aims are to:

(i) **support more Welsh language courses for adults.** You will need about £15 million.
(ii) **give £3 million for a new hospital in mid Wales.**
(iii) **reduce all primary school classes in Wales to less than 31.** Cost could be around £7 million.

Minister for Scotland

Your job is to protect Scottish interests. There is a need to build new housing in Glasgow and Edinburgh. You also have poor transport by train and want to improve it. Your aims are to:

(i) **get £100 million for new housing.**
(ii) **improve many railway lines and buy new trains.** At least £50 million needed.
(iii) **get about £20 million for a museum of Scottish life in London.** This will help English and other people to better understand how Scottish life is different to other parts of Britain *and* what unites them.

Resource 19 (continued)

Minister for Northern Ireland	Minister for Trade & Industry
Your job is to protect Irish interests but you also are responsible for an area where there is a civil war situation. The Catholic minority wants independence from Britain. But the Protestant majority wants to stay in the UK. Both sides have terrorist groups. Your aims are to: (i) **support poorer Catholic families by building better houses.** Cost will be £150 million. (ii) **build up police force to make Northern Ireland safer.** At least £40 million needed. (iii) **put money into joint Catholic and Protestant education projects.** You need about £25 million for this.	Your main priority is to reduce unemployment, poverty. This would also help to bring down crime figures. You are focusing on one main project. Your one aim, therefore, is to: (i) **start a fund for regional policy in poorer areas of Britain to reduce unemployment.** About £700 million needed for training and apprenticeships.

5 Rights, Responsibilities and the World Around Us

About this chapter

This chapter is about the rights and responsibilities of citizenship within the natural world. It begins by focusing on rights and how the enjoyment of these rights can affect others; in other words, global interdependency. Pupils learn about the citizenship aspects of sustainable development, including energy resources, waste disposal, transport, global, national and local targets. Pupils find out about the issues involved in sustainable farming and current debates such as animal transport. They find out about global famine and obesity, including the impact of fast food on our culture. The chapter also investigates how the design of the built environment enables access for disabled people. There are opportunities throughout to explore conflict resolution within a global and environmental perspective.

1. Rights, responsibilities and the environment

Activity A: What are our rights and responsibilities in the environment?

Target Group: Year 7

Learning Objectives
I should learn:

- About my rights in the physical world, e.g. shelter, food, warmth.
- That how I choose to live affects the lives of other people.
- What responsibilities I have towards the world around me.

Curriculum Links
Science: Greenhouse effect, radiation, ozone layer.
History: Rights and responsibilities, including the Universal Declaration of Human Rights.
Geography: Global interdependency, rising sea levels, deserted settlements, global warming.

Brainstorm with the pupils their rights – that is, what they *need* – regarding the environment: for example, the right to shelter, to food, to warmth, to make a livelihood.

Use the 'consequence map', see Resource 20, to explore how all people in the world are connected to each other and how the enjoyment of rights by one group can take away the rights of another group. The complete Consequence map could be shared with pupils. Or the beginning could be shown and pupils asked to complete it. Alternatively, cut up the different parts of the Consequence map and ask pupils to reassemble it using knowledge and understanding of science and geography.

Similar consequence maps can be produced for other concerns such as global warming causing deserts, consumption of petrol causing greenhouse gases, and so on. However, there are opportunities to explore these areas later in the chapter. In this chapter, the important learning aim is the idea of *global interdependency*.

Resource 20: Activity A: What are our rights and responsibilities in the environment?

Consequence Map

We have a RIGHT to be warm.

⇓

We want to be warm at home
so we have central heating.

⇓

Central heating is run on oil – it gets
its energy from the burning of oil.

⇓

When oil is burnt, gases escape into the air.
These are called 'greenhouse gases'.

⇓

They are called 'greenhouse gases' because they heat up the earth.
This is called 'global warming'.

⇓

Global warming causes ice to melt.
Huge icebergs melt in the Arctic and in Antarctica.

⇓

The melting of the ice causes sea levels to rise.
Over time this will cause whole islands in the
Pacific to be under water.

⇓

The people who live on these islands will lose their
RIGHTS to shelter, food, making a living, as well
as living their life as they have done for thousands of years.

Questions

Using the three headings below ask pupils to use information from the Consequence map or maps to show how what we need and want can conflict with the needs and wants of others.

- GOAL: What do we need and want?
- METHOD: What do we do to get it?
- EFFECT: How do our actions change other people's lives?

Look again at the Consequence map or maps. Ask pupils:
How could these problems be solved so that we are warm enough and the Pacific Islands survive?

For example, use of different fuels that do not cause global warming, wear more clothes, live more communally, put heating off at night, have laws about use of heating. Which ones might work best? Why? More local consequences could also be discussed, such as, desertification and the spread of diseases such as malaria.

Activity B: Do we need everything that we want? Do we have a right to everything that we want?

Target Group: Year 7

Learning Objectives
I should learn:

- About the differences between 'needs' and 'wants'.
- Why it is important to think about the differences.
- That everyone in the world cannot have what they want.

Resource 21: Activity B: Do we need everything that we want? Do we have a right to everything that we want?

Needs or Wants?

Live in a house	Have a washing machine
Be safe	Have enough food to live
Have heating on all the time	Have lots of money
Our community to be protected from any harm	Get taught well at school
Have a good shelter to live in	Have medicines and operations when I am sick
Have a television	Have a job
Have enough money to live on	Be listened to by others
Make a good living	Not to be bullied or picked on
Speak freely	Choose the rulers
Not do dirty or dangerous jobs	Meet with friends and have fun
Be private inside my own home	Go to school
Read books	Choose a job
Not to be put in prison without a fair trial	Have a big fridge

Cut out the cards. Ask pupils in pairs to sort the cards into 'Needs' and 'Wants'. They can also have a 'Not sure' group.

1. Ask each pair to give a 2 minute presentation:
   (i) Which were easy to decide?
   (ii) Which were difficult?
   (iii) Anything else they noticed or thought interesting or important?
2. Discuss with pupils:
   (i) What is the difference between needs and wants?
   (ii) Why is it important to think about the difference?
   (iii) Is there a difference between needs and *rights*?
   (iv) Do we have a right to all we need?
   (v) Do we have a right to all we want?

Do pupils agree or disagree with the statements below? Why? Why not?

- We cannot all have everything that we want.
- If some people have more, others have less.
- The world is full of things that can run out.
- We have responsibilities to take care of the rights of others.
- We do not have responsibilities towards others.
- Other people should look after themselves!
- We should take care of others because we need them to do the same for us!

Brainstorm with pupils:

(i) What are our rights regarding the environment?
(ii) What are our responsibilities regarding the environment?

Activity C: Do trees have rights too? What about the birds that live in them?

Target Group: Year 7

Learning Objectives
I should learn:

- About our rights and responsibilities regarding the environment.
- How human life is connected to and dependent on other life.
- That the choices we make affects all life.
- About species that have become extinct and endangered.

Curriculum Links
Design and Technology: Designing and making bird boxes.
Science: Birds and their habitats. Endangered and extinct species and the environment.
Geography: Settlements and their consequences including tree clearing.

Why do we need trees?
Discuss with pupils: 'Why do we need trees?'

In summary, we need trees to live because:

(i) Trees take in carbon dioxide and from it produce oxygen, which goes into the air, and carbon, which fixes in the wood and leaves, making wood a fuel and leaves a fertiliser for the soil.
(ii) Trees hold the earth together and stop the topsoil leaching away. They keep the land fertile.
(iii) Trees take a lot of water out of the soil. Therefore, if trees are taken away the soil becomes wetter and the land can become flooded.
(iv) Many animals, birds and insects live in trees. Many of these are essential for the health of other plants, including food crops.

What are the main threats to trees?

- Logging of trees (burnt to make way for new roads/housing/grazing land/food crops); paper and cardboard packaging.
- Pollution of air, including acid rain, temperature and rainfall changes caused by global warming.

What are the rights of the tree?
Pupils write a 'Declaration of the Rights of the Tree'. For example:

- the right not to be cut down without good reason and without being replaced;
- the right to breathe clean air;
- the right not to be acid rained on;

and so on.

Which birds have become extinct or endangered?
Pupils use resources of organisations, such as the RSPB, to find out which birds have already become extinct in the UK and which ones are endangered. Pupils could:

1. Write slogans for the protection of birds.
2. Find out what action is being taken locally to protect birds.
3. What could they themselves do to protect birds – in the school grounds? By raising awareness?

Taking Community Action!
There are opportunities here to develop the school grounds, including making bird nesting boxes within the Design and Technology curriculum.

2. All about rubbish!

Activity A: What will *we* leave behind?

Target Group: Years 7 to 8

Learning Objectives
I should learn:

- That every society leaves its own rubbish and its own 'environmental footprint'.
- That not all rubbish can be recycled or easily got rid of.
- That each year we, in the UK, make more and more rubbish.
- About national, local and school policies towards recycling.

Curriculum Links
Science: Organic and non-organic waste. Recycling of materials.
Geography: Impact of different settlements on the environment.
History: The use of archaeological and other sources of evidence about the past.

Every generation and society leaves behind its own 'environmental footprint'. What do the pupils think is meant by this? Draw on learning in history and geography to stimulate ideas. What environmental footprint was left by Stone Age people? By the enclosure of land in the eighteenth century? By the building of canals and trains in Victorian times?

What societies in the past have pupils found out about?

- Romans?
- Ancient Egyptians?
- Indus Valley people?
- Ancient Greeks?

What sort of rubbish and environmental footprints did they leave?
How is this rubbish useful to archaeologists and historians?
Is any of it harmful to us today?

What are we doing about our rubbish?
Pupils use Resource 22 to find out about rubbish. This information can be supplemented using organisations listed in the Useful Contacts section. Some of these organisations can also provide help and advice on taking action, as in Activity B below.

Resource 22: All about rubbish!

What is happening to rubbish in the UK and the rest of Europe?

- There is more and more of it. Each year the total amount of rubbish from our homes goes up by 3 per cent.
- Most of the rubbish is put in landfill sites (huge holes in the ground). These sites can make the surrounding land poisonous and can also poison the water.
- Some rubbish is recycled, for example, glass, paper and plastic can all be recycled. In 2002, 10 per cent of our rubbish was recycled.

What is the local picture about rubbish?

The recycling records of some local councils in England

Name of local council/borough	% of rubbish recycled in 1999
Dorset (County)	31
Eastleigh (Borough) (Hampshire)	26
Bournemouth (Borough)	24
Ashfield (Borough) (Nottinghamshire)	1
Corby (Borough) (Northamptonshire)	1
Mansfield (District) (Nottinghamshire)	1
Sedgefield (Borough) (Durham)	1
St Helens (Borough) (Lancashire)	1
Sunderland (City)	1

Source: Defra 2002

What does the government say?

- The British government has set a target that, by April 2006, England will be recycling 25 per cent of its rubbish.
- Under EU law, half the amount of rubbish that used to go into landfill in 1995 should, by 2009, be reused, composted or recycled. By 2016, this target rises to 65 per cent.

Questions

- What do you notice about councils in England and recycling rates?
- How near or how far are these councils from the targets for 2006?
- Brainstorm what sort of rubbish will be left by our generation.
  - What is 'biodegradable'? What isn't?
- What might our 'environmental footprint' look like?
  - Make a sketch of our generation's 'Rubbish Mountain'.

Activity B: Rubbish: Recycle, Reuse, Reduce!

Target Group: Years 7 to 8

Learning Objectives
I should learn:

- Why it is important to reuse, recycle and reduce rubbish.
- How I can help by changing what I do with rubbish.
- My rights and responsibilities towards world resources.

Curriculum Links
Numeracy: Using and interpreting percentage rates.
Science: Organic, non-organic materials.
Geography: Local environmental policies about rubbish.

Taking Community Action!

What happens to rubbish in our area?
Pupil research rubbish policy in the local area. For example:

- What is the current recycling rate of the local council?
- What are the local issues regarding rubbish and the environment?
- What happens to rubbish from school? From home?
- Does the school recycle any rubbish? Is home rubbish recycled?

Pupils could do a 'Rubbish Analysis' either at school or home.
Examine the contents of one day's rubbish.

- How much is recyclable?
- How much is reusable?
- How much is neither recyclable nor reusable?
- What can be done with this rubbish?

How can the amount of rubbish be reduced:

- at home?
- at school?

Write a 'Rubbish Policy' for home or school.
For example:

- What could be reused (envelopes, paper, cardboard)?
- What could be recycled?
- How could we make less rubbish?

3. Rights, responsibilities and sustainable development

Activity A: What is sustainable development?

Target Group: Years 8 to 9

Learning Objectives
I should learn:

- What is meant by 'sustainable development' and why it is important today.
- About national and global policies towards the environment.
- To use terms correctly that are relevant to sustainable development and the environment.

Curriculum Links
Numeracy: Reading graphs.
Geography: Ecosystems, energy resources, sustainable development.
Science: Energy resources, Energy and Electricity.
Design and Technology: Design and make a board game on sustainable development.

Sustainable development
Means 'ensuring a better quality of life for everyone now and for generations to come'. Share this definition with pupils (see Resource 23). What are the two most important words in this definition given? Pupils write out the meaning in their own words, with illustrations if they wish.

In order to have sustainable development, therefore, we need to:

- Make sure all people in the world have what they need for a good life.
- Protect the environment from damage.
- Use natural resources carefully so that they do not run out.

Hand out or display Resource 23. Pupils read and complete.

Resource 23: Activity A: What is sustainable development?

Terms and their meanings

Sustainable development
Ensuring a better quality of life for everyone now and for generations to come.

Renewable energy resources
Sources of energy that can be replaced over a short period of time – that is, hydro-electric (making energy from water movement). They can make themselves again in a short period of time.

Fossil fuels
Fuels which have been made over a very long time, that is millions of years, from organic matter – dead plants and animals. Coal, gas, oil are all non-renewable energy resources.

Fossil fuels have taken a long time to be made and are, therefore, non-renewable energy resources. They cannot make themselves again. Once they are used they are gone. Gas is a fossil fuel.

Fuel
Substance that releases energy when it is chemically changed, usually by burning. For example, coal is burnt to release energy.

Questions
(i) What is the most important difference between a renewable and a non-renewable energy resource?
(ii) Write a definition of 'non-renewable energy resources'.

Sorting Exercise
Sort the following into renewable and non-renewable energy resources:

Wind	Human and animal sewage
Solar	Fast growing willow trees
Slow growing oak trees	Oil
Nuclear	Fast growing sugar cane
Gas	Coal
Tidal and wave flows	

Activity B: How can we make sustainable development happen?

Target Group: Years 8 to 9

Learning Objectives
I should learn:

- About national and global policies towards sustainable development.
- The challenges of making sustainable development happen.

Curriculum Links
Science: Renewable and non-renewable resources, energy, organic matter.
Geography: 'Developed' and developing' countries, politics of sustainable development.

What is involved in having global sustainable development?
Display or hand out the spray diagram on sustainable development (Resource 24). Pupils use it to stimulate their thinking about the issues involved in having sustainable development. What can they add to the diagram? What other questions will need to be asked? What other issues need to be thought about? Can they add any 'answers' or 'solutions'?

Use Resource 25 to find out about national and global policies towards sustainable development and the challenges involved.

Resource 24: Activity B: How can we make sustainable development happen?

Spray diagram: sustainable development

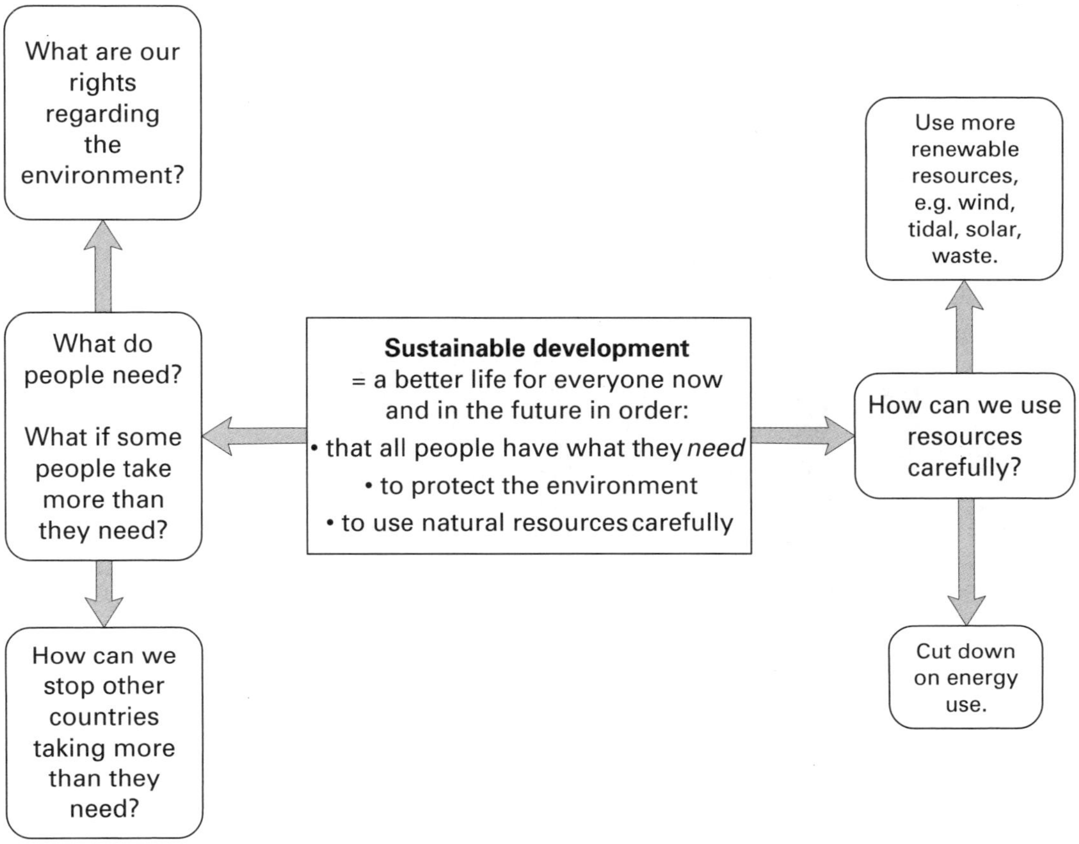

Resource 25: Activity B: How can we make sustainable development happen?

Information Sheet: Energy resources

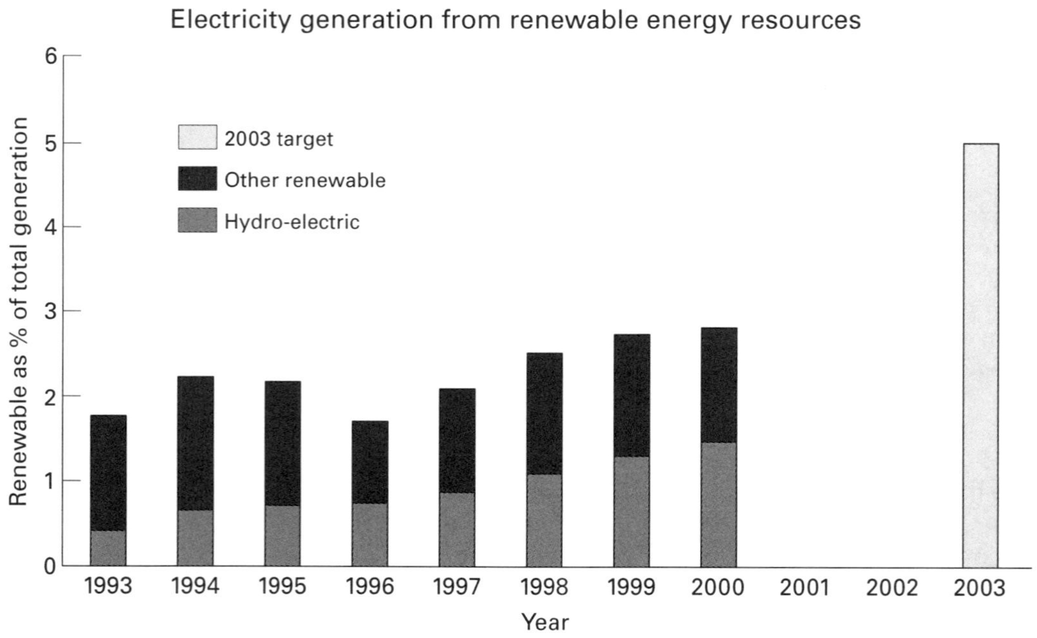

(*Source: Directory of Energy Resources 2001*, DTI)

What is government energy policy in the UK?

The government has a target of 5 per cent of electricity being generated from renewable fuels by 2003. By 2010 its target is 10 per cent.
The government has other targets:

- Electricity suppliers have to get an increasing proportion of electricity from renewable energy resources.
- Electricity from non-renewable energy resources will have to pay a special tax called the 'Climate Change Levy'.
- Special grants of money will go towards developing renewable resources.

Questions

Study the graph above.
What is the current level of use of renewable energy resources to make electricity?
What is the government's target?
What observations can you make from this graph?
Look at the government's three other targets.
In pairs, work out how each will help to make sustainable development happen.

Global policy

The Kyoto Protocol (agreement) of 2001 aimed at making sustainable development happen across the world. The Kyoto agreement recognised the importance of having a global as well as a national policy on development. Developed countries met together in 2002 to talk about sustainable development, including reducing carbon emissions (caused by burning fuel for energy). They agreed to cut back CO2 emissions to 1990 levels (21,500 million tons emitted globally) until 2008, then to cut back levels even more from 2008 onwards. However, there were a number of problems that could be discussed by teachers and pupils. For example:

- The USA refused to sign the agreement. The USA uses a disproportionately higher amount of fossil fuel energy than other countries.
- What should be done about developed and developing countries? Should some be allowed to emit more carbon than others?
- What should be done about hotter and colder countries? Should colder countries be allowed to emit more carbon than hotter countries?

Write a letter to the President of the USA explaining why it is important that:

(a) All countries sign the agreement.
(b) The USA in particular signs the agreement.

Taking Community Action!
Science Fair: organise a Science Fair at school. This could be a display of energy saving devices and/or an exhibition on how recycling works.

How can we teach younger children about sustainable development?
Design a 'Sustainable Development' board game. The aims are to help children and adults learn about sustainable development: its meaning, aims, challenges. The game should be:

- Interesting
- Fun
- For ages 11 and up
- For between two to six players

Activity C: How can we make a difference? What are the challenges? TRANSPORT!

Target Group: Years 8 to 9

Learning Objectives
I should learn:

- The challenges of making sustainable development happen.
- How some values (what we think is important) conflict with some goals of sustainable development.
- How to resolve conflict.

Curriculum Links:
Drama: Using drama to explore conflicts and conflict resolution.
Science: Greenhouse effect, renewable and non-renewable energy resources.
Geography: Transport, public and private, and settlements.

Two different activities are offered below to raise awareness of the possibilities for action and the challenges involved.

TRANSPORT
Put pupils in groups. Allocate the six roles set out on cards in Resource 26. Give the groups some time to prepare their characters. *Either* ask pupils to prepare a short drama which shows:

- Goals of each character (what they all want)
- Values of each character (what they all think is important)
- Rights and responsibilities
- Conflict between them/how they disagree
- What they have in common
- Possible solutions

Or 'hot seat' (question) each character to draw out each of the above points.

The spray diagram on sustainable development (Resource 24) will help pupils contextualise the role play within the debate about rights and the environment. Encourage pupils to add to their characters, including solutions such as improved public transport, private car tax scheme (as in London), home delivery of food, shared car use, tax on motorways, and so on.

After the role play, discuss what the pupils have learnt about sustainable development and transport. Make a list of their learning outcomes.

Taking Community Action!

Tell the pupils that the government set a target of reducing carbon dioxide levels by 20 per cent on 1990 levels by 2010. However, in both years 2001 and 2002, carbon dioxide levels increased.

Pupils write a letter to a local MP or local councillor asking about current carbon dioxide levels and making suggestions about how to reduce them.

Resource 26: Activity C: How can we make a difference? What are the challenges? TRANSPORT

Role play: Transport

YOU are a LORRY DRIVER You want to keep your job. You work for a supermarket chain that needs to transport food around the UK. You do long haul journeys. You are worried that if a tax on petrol goes up or other restrictions on traffic are introduced, you might lose your job.	**YOU are a SENIOR CITIZEN** You are 80 years of age and have difficulty walking unaided. You have a car for going to the shops and seeing your friends. You do short, local journeys and need to park near the place you are visiting. You live on a small pension and could not afford to pay a penny more on petrol.
YOU are an ENVIRONMENTAL ACTIVIST You care about the world around you. You want the government to make changes for sustainable development. These changes include more tax on petrol and diesel, better public transport, more hydrogen and/or battery-operated vehicles, more bicycle use, restricted car use in town.	**YOU are a PARENT of FOUR CHILDREN** You have four children – two at a local primary school and two at a local secondary school. You also have a job which you need to get to by 9.30 a.m. You are often late and your boss gets cross. Sometimes you do the family shopping in your lunch break.
YOU are a TEENAGER You live outside town but you like to visit at weekends to see your friends and go to the local Youth Club. Your parents only let you go on condition that they take you and pick you up so that they know you are safe. You have a bicycle but your parents won't let you ride it on the road at night. At school there is nowhere to park it safely.	**YOU are a LOCAL COUNCILLOR** You want to keep everyone happy – partly because you need their votes in order to remain a councillor. Your council has targets about sustainable development that include reducing the amount of pollution from cars. Many people are complaining about traffic jams. Some are asking for more roads and a bypass around the town to ease traffic. Others are asking for better public transport, including a tram system.

Activity D: How can we make a difference? What are the challenges? ENERGY AT HOME!

Target Group: Years 8 to 9

Learning Objectives
I should learn:

- The challenges of making sustainable development happen.
- How to do an investigation into energy use at home.

How much energy do we use at home?
Tell pupils that they are going to keep an 'Energy Diary'. This will involve recording their use of energy over a 24-hour period, preferably at the weekend.

Brainstorm all possible uses of energy at home through 24 hours. For example:

- Running water
- Night lights
- Central heating
- Electric lights
- Washing machine
- Fridge
- Kettle
- Dishwasher
- Microwave
- Television, video
- Computer

Pupils will need:

- Record Sheet
- List of energy uses
- Watch/clock/stopwatch
- Pen

Use the diaries to work out some ways of saving energy in the home.

The website *www.carboncalculator.org.uk* will measure the impact of energy use in your own home. Energy saving tips can be found at *www.saveenergy.co.uk*, *www.theecologist.org* and *www.globalactionplan.org.uk*. Other useful organisations are listed in the Useful Contacts section.

British Gas produces resources and runs competitions to do with saving energy in the home.

Pupils design a pamphlet called 'HOME ENERGY: HOW TO SAVE OUR PLANET!' This could be distributed to parents, carers and others within the local community.

Activity E: What can we do? What will we do?

Target Group: Years 8 to 9

Learning Objectives
I should learn:

- To weigh up our ideas: Are they possible? Will they make a difference? How?
- To use our thinking to reach judgements and make choices.
- To take positive action/to make a difference locally for the world.
- To understand why it is important to think about people's values when trying to make changes.

Curriculum Links
Science: Sustainable development, energy, fuel, waste, renewable and non-renewable resources.
Geography: Environmental practice and policy. Ecosystems and the school grounds.
Design and Technology: Surveying and designing the built environment for sustainable development.

Brainstorm all the changes that could be made at school to help to save the environment. For example:

- Ride bicycles to school
- Recycle, reduce, reuse waste at school
- Turn the heating down at school
- Stop parents driving to school
- Put up a wind farm for energy for school
- Burn local chicken manure for energy for school
- Save rainwater for toilets and washing machines
- Stop teachers driving to school
- Use lagging and foil to reduce heat loss
- Switch lights off when possible
- Plant trees in the school grounds
- Run an Information campaign

Ask pupils to consider each idea in relation to the following questions:

(i) What are our goals regarding the environment?
(ii) How will each action make a difference?
  - A positive (good) difference for the environment?

- Other differences?
- Will our action have any negative consequences?

(iii) Is it possible? Will it work?
(iv) How could we do it?

- What skills, materials and attitudes would we need?

(v) What is the situation now?
(vi) What would need to change?

Pupils could brainstorm the above using a spray diagram structure.

Point out to pupils that a 'difference' could be a negative one. For example, turning the heating down might make pupils too cold to be able to attend to learning. Teachers might bring in their own heaters that use more energy than the school central heating. Burning chicken manure could be very dangerous for air quality and health.

Pupils will need more information to pursue all the above questions in greater depth. The Useful Contacts pages give contact details for informative organisations, including one giving details on a wind-powered school.

Taking Community Action!
Write a School Energy Policy.

(i) Who will need to be consulted? Why? How?
(ii) What will we need:

- to know (information)
- to be able to do (skills)
- to have (materials, resources)
- to feel and think about (attitudes).

(iii) Who can help?, i.e. who can provide appropriate

- Skills
- Knowledge
- Materials/resources
- Attitudes

(iv) What happens if pupils and teachers break the policy?
(v) How will we know if the policy is making a difference?

4. Food, farming and famine

Activity A: What is the countryside for?

Target Group: Years 8 to 9

Learning Objectives
I should learn:

- The different uses of the countryside.
- The relationship between town and countryside in modern Britain.
- Challenges facing rural communities and rural areas.

Curriculum Links
Geography: Settlements, town and countryside planning and development.

Either use the spray diagram (Resource 24) or use ideas from the pupils to build up a similar spray diagram.

Resource 27: Activity A: What is the countryside for?

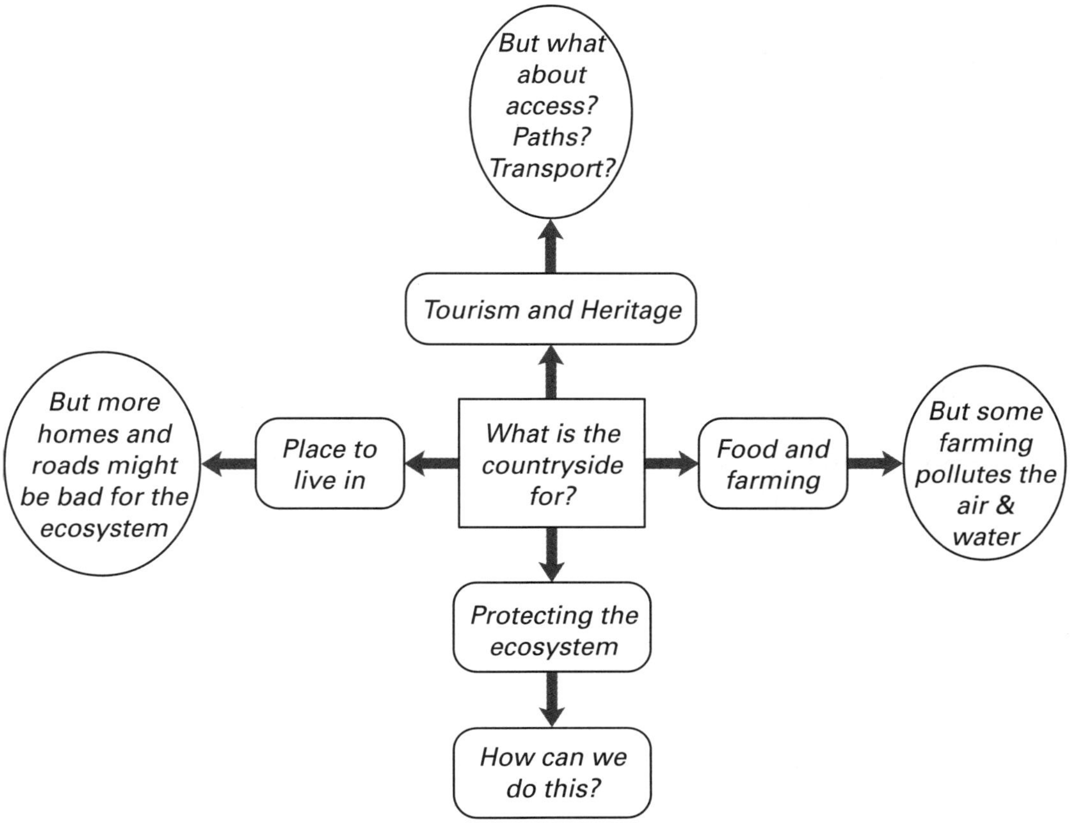

Activity B: What is sustainable farming?

Target Group: Years 8 to 9

Learning Objectives
I should learn:

- About the different ways of farming (growing food).
- Advantages and disadvantages of 'extensive' and 'intensive' farming.
- About sustainable farming methods.

Curriculum Links
Geography: Food and farming. Sustainable development. Extensive and intensive farming methods.

Brainstorm with pupils what they know about farming in Britain. It is possible that urban pupils in particular will have little knowledge and understanding of farming and may stereotype or generalise farming. The following basic information can be used to address stereotypes and build up a more accurate picture as a starting point for discussion.

- In 2001 the average farmer's annual wage was £5,200.
- The average age of a farmer is 57 years old.
- Most farmers work 60+ hours per week.
- Britain has the highest standards of animal welfare in the world, especially for pigs. This makes British meat more expensive than many other countries' meat.
- In 2002 Britain was 70 per cent self-sufficient in foodstuffs.
- Organic farming is rapidly increasing but still only accounted for 1 per cent of total food consumption in Britain in 2002.
- Many farmers supplement their income with tourism, e.g. B & B.
- There is huge diversity within the farming community, ranging from small hill farmers (sheep) to large arable farmers.
- Farmers had one of the highest suicide rates for any occupation in Britain in 2002.

Discuss with pupils the differences between 'extensive' farming (few animals/crops, spread out, longer life, slower growth, non-factory, more likely to be free range and/organic) and 'intensive' farming (factory farming, fast growth, more likely to use antibiotics, non-organic fertilisers, pesticides).

Write up the different features and ask pupils to think of advantages and disadvantages of both methods.

Questions
Which farming method is more likely to support sustainable development? Why?
Which farming method is less likely to support sustainable development?

Why?
Which method is likely to make meat more expensive?
Which method is likely to make meat less expensive?
Which farming method is kinder to animals? Why?

Resource 28: Activity B: What is sustainable farming?

Solutions for sustainable farming?

Think about the list of possible 'solutions' below. Tick the columns A, B, C, D as appropriate.
Tick A for solutions which might support sustainable farming.
Tick B for solutions which might not.
Tick C for solutions which are also supportive of sustainable development.
Tick D for solutions which are not.

You can tick more than one column.
You may need to think 'laterally'. For example, 'More local markets selling local produce' would mean fewer lorries on the road therefore less air pollution and better animal welfare. You could tick column C.

Possible 'solution'?	A	B	C	D
People eat less meat, less often				
People pay more for meat but less for vegetables and fruit				
More local markets selling local produce (food)				
More supermarkets selling global and national produce				
People only eat food in season				
All land to be farmed organically				
All land to be farmed intensively				
More selling of food via mail order and the Internet				
Farmers to be given money for having fewer animals on land				
Farmers to be given money for having more animals on land				
Less packaging of food				
More packaging of food				

Write a Declaration of Rights for

- Farmers
- Animals
- Consumers (shoppers and eaters!)

Activity C: Dilemmas and choices in the world of farming

Target Group: Years 8 to 9

Learning Objectives
I should learn:

- About some of the dilemmas and choices that face farmers and consumers (buyers).
- To weigh up and judge different arguments.
- To take part in discussion.
- That knowing more can help me make up or change my mind about important questions.

Should we or shouldn't we?
Hand out Resource Sheets 29 and 30 below.
Some of the points made may be misleading. Which ones might be misleading? What information/'evidence' needs to be checked? How could this be done? What other information would they like to know? Who or what might help them? Which arguments do they agree and disagree with?

Can pupils add to the arguments on either side? In groups of three pupils prepare a role play. One pupil on each 'side' and one who faces the dilemma. Alternatively pupils can prepare their arguments and then be questioned. Take a class vote on the issue at the beginning and at the end. Did any pupils change their mind? Why? Why not?

Resource 29: Activity C: Dilemmas and choices in the world of farming

Should we or shouldn't we . . . Transport animals

Animal transport abroad is an important source of income for Britain. We'll lose money if we don't do it.	Animal transport is stressful and cruel for animals. They travel very long distances in cramped lorries without fresh food and water.
Animal transport means we eat fresher food because it hasn't been dead so long. That's better for health.	We don't need to transport animals to eat fresh food. Instead we can buy local food at local markets and shops.
Animal transport is very important for supermarkets because they sell so much produce around the country.	Supermarkets could be made to sell only local meat.
Animal transport means consumers have more choice of fresh meat. They can eat British lamb in France and German beef in Britain.	Animal transport is very bad for the environment because of the fuel that is used and the carbon emissions.
To be self-sufficient in food, Britain would not have free trade. This would upset other countries.	Britain does not need to import or export animals. It could be self-sufficient in food.

Resource 30: Activity C: Dilemmas and choices in the world of farming

Should we or shouldn't we . . . Ban fox hunting

Hunting of foxes is cruel. The fox is terrified.	Foxes kill chickens and sheep. That's bad for farmers and cruel for farm animals. Often a fox will kill all the chickens but only eat one.
Hunting is cruel because the fox gets chased for miles and torn apart.	Hounds go for the neck and the fox dies instantly, in seconds.
Farmers can always shoot or poison foxes.	If hunting is banned, some farmers will shoot or poison foxes instead. That's more cruel and poison harms other animals. Being killed by another animal is more natural for foxes.
Hunting is not working anyway. There is little evidence it keeps down fox numbers.	Fox numbers are on the rise. This is because there are more conifer forests, more sheep and fewer shepherds.
More foxes die on roads than by hunting. There's no point.	Most foxes killed by hunts are male, not female, and old. This is good for the foxes, because it keeps down disease, as well as being good for the farmers.
Foxes get very stressed by being hunted. One fox rescued from a hunt had blood in its urine.	Hunting is not allowed in the breeding season.
Hunting of foxes should not be a sport. People should not enjoy hunting.	Hunting has been a chance for rural communities to get together throughout history. It is an important social event and part of the culture of the countryside.
In a MORI poll in March 2002, 62 per cent of people supported a ban. The poll asked a representative group of the population.	Most people in Britain are not farmers but live in towns. They don't understand hunting. Research by the National Farmers' Union showed most farmers support hunting.
Farmers are a small minority in Britain and shouldn't be listened to.	Farmers are a small minority in Britain and their rights should be protected.
Foxes kill rabbits which do lots of damage to farm crops. Therefore we need foxes.	Let farmers decide what should happen on their own farms. They know best.

Activity D: Fat and Famine: A fairer world or a fatter world?

Target Group: Years 8 to 9

Learning Objectives
I should learn:

- How famine and obesity co-exist in the world.
- The cost of obesity to individuals and the country and the world.
- Why obesity is a social not a personal problem.

Curriculum Links
Food technology: Junk food, healthy eating, politics of food.
Geography: Global interdependence, sustainable development, food and farming.
PHSE: Health, eating, body image and self-esteem.

Tell pupils that fat (obesity) and famine co-exist at the same time. While some people die of hunger, others die of obesity and the illnesses it causes. Both fat and famine are increasing problems in different parts of the world. In the USA, 60 per cent of Americans were fat or obese in 2002. Cinema and aeroplane seats were being expanded. In Britain, 20 per cent of adults and 13 per cent of children were obese in 2002 and the figures were increasing very quickly. By 2010 obesity has been predicted to affect one in four people in the world. In some countries, e.g. Samoa, fat and famine co-exist.

Obesity can be very dangerous because being fat can make it much more likely to suffer heart disease, diabetes and other diseases. Some people who are fat are suffering from malnutrition because they eat food high in fat but low in nutrients. In areas of famine, thin and starving people are often also suffering from malnutrition.

Obesity is not necessarily an individual problem but a social problem. That means it is caused by the way the whole society lives, not just the individual person. For example, the way of life in western 'developed' capitalist countries like the USA and Britain can cause people to be obese because of junk food, cars, adverts for sweets and fizzy drinks and so on. In fact, studies in the early twenty-first century showed that obesity spread with the spread of junk food from the 1970s onwards. Resource 31 can be used for information and discussion about junk food.

The following list shows some trends in British society. How might each one contribute towards obesity?

- People work longer hours. Less time to cook.
- Adverts glorify sweets, fizzy drinks, 'junk food'.
- More children travel longer distances to school in cars.

- Fewer children attend local schools that they can walk to.
- Many playing fields and parks are being used for housing.
- Increase in the number of 'fast food' outlets, including vending machines.

Tell pupils, organised into small groups, that they are panels of experts called by the government to draft a **10 Point Action Plan: 'Reducing Obesity for the Health of the Nation'**. They must begin with a short paragraph (maximum 150 words) explaining why obesity is bad for the environment, bad for the NHS and bad for sustainable farming. Possible points for their action plan could include:

- Tax fatty foods
- Build more sports centres
- Ban cars to school
- Shorten working day
- Make Food Science compulsory for all up to 16 years.

Note: This activity could cause sensitivity in the classroom towards pupils and teachers who are obese and/or anorexic and/or who have a negative body image. Teachers may wish to start with ground rules for discussion (see Appendix C) and by overtly and explicitly discussing prejudice against fat people. Such a discussion could be supported by images from the media which show the 'ideal' body image. This 'ideal' body image also could be discussed in terms of its health implications, for example, possible link to increasing rates of anorexia, bulimia in boys and girls. Teachers may also wish to explicitly raise the gender dimension of body image, food and obesity. In all cases it is important to stress the social causes of illness around weight rather than personal or individual causes. This can be a powerful and empowering learning experience for young people.

Resource 31: Activity D: Fat and Famine: A fairer world or a fatter world?

Are burgers bad for us?

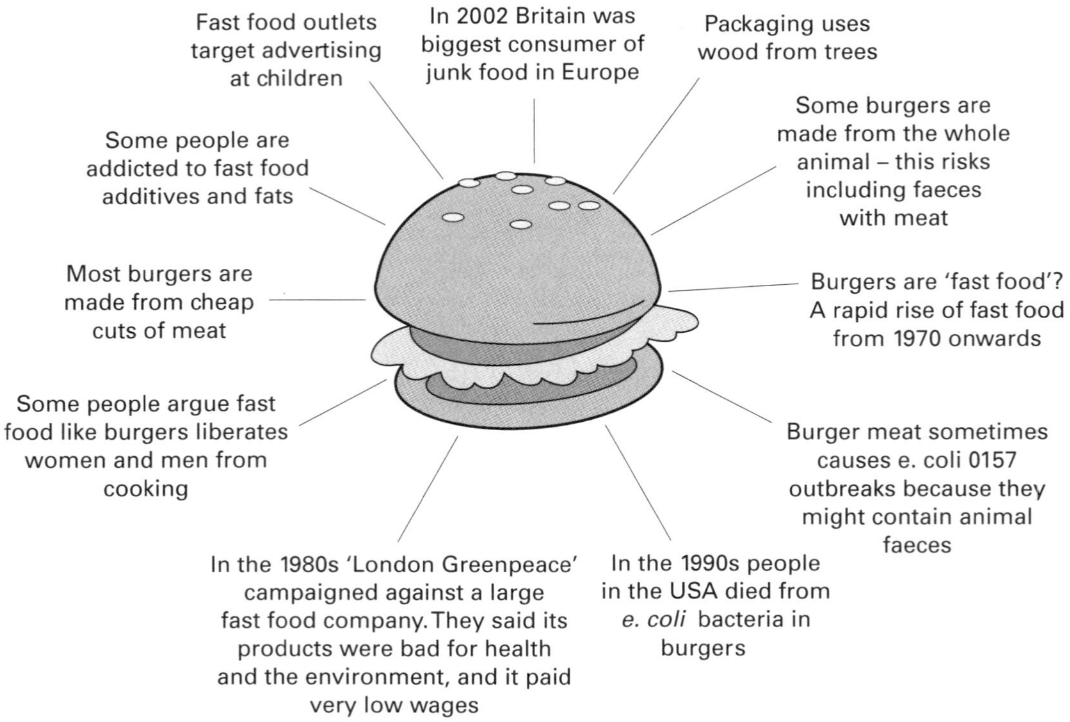

5. Science, people and dilemmas

Activity A: Should we or shouldn't we?

Target Group: Year 9

Learning Objectives
I should learn:

- About some of the dilemmas raised by scientific knowledge.
- How science can change lives.
- Uses and abuses of science in our society.
- To weigh up and judge different arguments.
- To take part in discussion.
- That knowing more can help me make up or change my mind about important questions.

Should we or shouldn't we?
Hand out Resource 32. Some of the points made may be misleading. Which ones might be misleading? What information/'evidence' needs to be checked? How could this be done? What other information would they like to know? Who or what might help them? Can pupils add to the arguments on either side?

In groups of three, pupils prepare a role play. One pupil on each 'side' and one who faces the dilemma. Alternatively pupils can prepare their arguments and then be questioned. Take a class vote on the issue at the beginning and at the end. Did any pupils change their mind? Why? Why not?

This model can be used with a range of scientific 'dilemmas'. For example:

- Genetic engineering
- Cloning
- Fertility treatment
- Animal testing

Resource 32: Activity A: Should we or shouldn't we?

Should we or shouldn't we . . . Immunise children

Government says vaccinations are safe and a good idea.	Some people, especially homeopaths and parents of autistic children, worry that vaccinations cause serious health problems.
Children can die of diseases such as measles, meningitis and TB if not vaccinated.	The MMR (measles, mumps, rubella) vaccination was launched in 1988. In 1987 in the UK there were only six deaths from measles out of 42,165 cases.
Government has said the increase in autism is not to do with MMR but because of other factors, including better diagnosis.	Autism has increased sharply since MMR was introduced in 1988. Many parents and some doctors think there might be a link.
Many children cannot fight diseases on their own and can be killed or impaired by measles, rubella, polio, etc.	Some people, including homeopathic doctors, believe it is better to get diseases than to vaccinate. Vaccination means the body does not learn to fight infections by itself.
Vaccinations are life saving. Many lives have been saved from TB, meningitis, measles, rubella, etc.	Some people believe vaccinations cause other diseases such as asthma, cancer, bowel problems, etc.
Research done at London's Royal Free and University College hospitals said there was no scientific evidence of a link between MMR and autism.	Most medical research is funded by drug companies. They make a lot of money from vaccinations. They are *not* going to say that vaccinations are bad!

6. Rights, disability and the built environment

Activity A: What are the environmental issues for people with physical impairments?

Target Group: Years 8 to 9

Learning Objectives
I should learn:

- About the built environment and the rights of physically impaired people.
- Government policy towards impairment and disability.
- The words 'impaired' and 'disabled' and how they are used.

Curriculum Links
Design and Technology: Design of built environment, design of environment and technology for supporting rights of disabled people.
Geography: Access and the built environment.
Literacy: Use of language.

Why is it important to think about language and 'labels'?
Discuss the use of the terms 'disabled' and 'impaired'.
What reactions do pupils have to them?
What is meant by 'dis-abled'?

Suggest this way of thinking:

> 'Impairment' is a physical feature that someone has, e.g. cannot walk unaided.
> 'Disabled' is what happens to them in certain places and situations. For example, they become 'disabled' when they need to get into a building which has a step.

What messages are being sent by describing a person's condition as an 'impairment' and only using 'disabled' about an action they want to take but cannot because of the way their environment is built?

How does the local environment
(i) Disable
and
(ii) enable
people with impairments?

Teachers may want to offer pupils 'hands on' experience of moving around the local environment with an impairment. For example, do a blind walk; borrow a wheelchair from the local hospital.

Alternatively, get pupils in groups to move around the school and/or the wider local environment. Allocate different impairment challenges (walking, hearing, seeing) to different groups. They should consider which parts of the environment might cause problems. For example, stairs, pedestrian crossings, kerbs, cash point machines, public telephones. Which signals within the school and local environment might also be challenging? For example, school bell, car horn.

Talk about:
What parts of the environment make a sight-impaired person 'disabled'?
What parts of the environment make a walking-impaired person 'disabled'?
What parts of the environment make a hearing-impaired person 'disabled'?

Ask pupils what can be seen and heard at a pedestrian crossing (beeps, flashing figures, tactile paving, ramped kerb). What is the function of each of these? Why are they important?

(*Note:* Tactile paving are paving slabs with raised circles on them that can be felt while walking.)

Make a plan of the streets around the school.
How many pedestrian crossings are there?
How many have the features listed above?

Hand out Resource 33 to pupils. Read, and then do the activity at the end.

Resource 33: Activity A: What are the environmental issues for people with physical impairments?

I can't get in!: Disability and access
Information and Action!

What is the law about disability and access?
By October 2004 all businesses (laundrettes, shops, lawyers, offices, etc.) must have access for disabled people. Disabled people must be able to get in and use their services.

What about schools and transport?
Everywhere doesn't have to change.
Schools, colleges, universities do not have to provide such access.
Buses and trains do not have to provide access.

What do some disabled people think about this?
Some are worried about whether the law will actually be obeyed. They think businesses will break the law. If they do, disabled people who cannot use their services may have to take them to court themselves to force them obey the law. But taking someone to court is very expensive and many disabled people are unemployed or on low incomes.

Ruba Sivagnanam of Radar, the disability network says: 'For most disabled people, accessible public transport would make the biggest difference to their everyday lives.'

What do local businesses know and do about disability?
Many businesses want to change. Some want to change because by not having disabled access they are losing lots of customers and therefore lots of money. For example, Direct Line, a telephone banking service, is used by many sight-impaired and walking-impaired people who cannot easily get to a bank. It makes money because it gives easy access.

However, a study in 2002 by the Disability Rights Commission (DRC) found that many businesses did not understand enough about disability to make the right changes: for example, many had put in ramps and lifts but had done nothing for sight-impaired and hearing-impaired people. In fact less than 5 per cent of disabled people use a wheelchair. Most have other different disabilities.

Another problem the DRC found was that many businesses have done nothing towards achieving the government target for 2004. Some are saying it is too expensive. Small businesses can get some help with paying for changes.

Find out:
What are businesses planning to do in your area?
How much do they know about disability?
How much do they know about the law?

Write a pamphlet to help one local business make changes. *Include:*
Information about disabled people (what disabled people want, statistics, types of disability).
Specific problems in the local environment.

Carry out an 'Access Survey' of local businesses.
Present the findings.

6 All about the Media

About this chapter

The area of investigating and analysing the mass media, and issues related to it, is dealt with throughout this book. In each chapter, 1 to 5, there are opportunities within activities to use the media both as a source of information and to investigate attitudes, opinions, values and beliefs about a range of citizenship issues, including human rights, British identity, crime, justice, environmental concerns, ethical dilemmas, power, politics, and so on. The focus in this chapter, therefore, is on discrete activities that can be used to teach pupils about the nature of information within a variety of media, the power of information and restrictions on freedom of information and, last but not least, the importance of being critical thinkers in relation to the mass media.

1. What is news?

Activity A: What's on the front page?

Target Group: Year 7

Learning Objectives
I should learn:

- About differences and similarities between British newspapers.
- How to investigate the front page of newspapers.
- Why and how different newspapers design their front page look.

Curriculum Links
Literacy: Comprehension of headlines and newspaper articles.
Numeracy: Measuring, calculating percentages.
History: Using newspapers as a source of information in an investigation.

Depending on the nature of the content, a wide range of other subject areas could be drawn upon.

In groups, pupils analyse the front page of a wide range of newspapers, including local, regional, national, broadsheets and tabloids. They analyse the newspapers using the table in Resource 34.

After pupils have completed Resource 34, display and discuss their findings. For example:

What do the pupils notice about:

1. Type of newspaper and main subject matter?
2. Type of newspaper and other factors, such as number of words?
3. What conclusions and judgements can the pupils make about 'What's on the front page?'

Resource 34: Activity A: What's on the front page?

Newspaper title	Type – for example: Local; Regional; National; Broadsheet; Tabloid	Actual size of front page (cm)	Number of head-lines

Resource 34 (continued)

Total size of space taken up by headlines (cm & %)	Number of articles	Total size of space taken up by articles (cm & %)	Approximate number of words on page	Font size of articles	Main subject matter of articles – for example Crime Sport Politics etc.

Activity B: What makes 'news'? What doesn't?

Target Group: Years 7 to 8

Learning Objectives
I should learn:

- How to analyse use of language in newspapers.
- About the attitudes and beliefs of different newspapers.

Curriculum Links
Literacy: Comprehension and analysis of language, including consideration of audience and purpose.
Numeracy: Measuring, calculating percentages.
History: Using newspapers as a source of information in an investigation. Detecting and analysing opinion, fact, choice of language, in relation to audience and purpose. Interpretation and representation.

Depending on the nature of the content, a wide range of subject areas could be drawn upon.

Refer back to and build on Activity A. In groups, using Resource 34, pupils apply the methodology used in Activity A to the whole content of a range of newspapers. They then divide up a number of main or significant articles between them and carry out a content analysis of each article using the structure of Resource 35.

Resource 35 is on pp. 132–133.

Resource 35: Activity B: What makes 'news'? What doesn't?

Newspaper title	Headline of article	Where article appears (page & position)	Brief summary of article

Resource 35 (continued)

Number of sentences/% that are 'opinion/belief/ interpretation/ judgement'	Number of sentences/% that are/contain 'fact'	Summarise how audience is supposed to feel on reading the article	How are these feelings built up by the choice of language? Select words and phrases to demonstrate ideas.

Activity C: What can we learn from the mass media about our society?

Target Group: Years 7 to 8

Learning Objectives
I should learn:

- About the different forms of media today.
- How the media changed people's lives in the twentieth century.
- About the opportunities offered by, as well as the dangers of using, different media.
- To use the media critically.

Curriculum Links
Literacy: Language, purpose, impact and audience. Being a critical 'reader'.
History: Using newspapers as a source of information in an investigation.
Design and Technology: Technological change in the twentieth century.

Brainstorm with pupils all the different sources of information that make up the mass media, including radio, television, newspapers, the Internet. Build up a spray diagram of basic information in response to the questions:

(i) When was this media form invented and first used?
(ii) How did it change people's lives?: including:
- Men
- Women
- 'Housebound' people
- Children
- Senior citizens

(iii) What languages are used in this media form?
(iv) Is it local/national/global?
(v) What is its main purpose/purposes? To entertain? To inform? To persuade? To make money?
(vi) How do the purposes affect the product?
(vii) What opportunities does it offer?
(viii) What dangers does it have?

Pupils write a list of 'How to use the media: Do's and Don'ts'.
Pupils could be allocated, in small groups, a different media form each.

Points for their list could include:
DO find out when this was made/written.
DO find out who wrote it.
DO separate fact and interpretation.
DON'T believe everything you read . . .

Taking Community Action!
The pupils' 'How to use the media: Do's and Don'ts' lists could support critical thinkers throughout the school by being displayed in computer rooms, by newspapers, in the library, etc.

Where pupils feel strongly about specific concerns, they could write letters to media organisations, MPs, consumer rights groups and so on.

2. Who owns information?

Activity A: How powerful is 'the word'? How free is 'the word'?

Target Group: Year 9

Learning Objectives
I should learn:

- How 'democracy' is limited by the media and who owns the media.
- About the aims, methods, achievements of individuals and organisations who have taken action or are taking action for freedom of speech.
- How I can take action to support freedom of speech and information.

Curriculum Links
Literacy: Power and the control of language. Editing a piece of prose for a particular purpose.
History: Democracy, freedom of speech and limitations on political and social rights. Resistance, change and the role of the individual. Nazi and communist dictatorships, censorship and propaganda.

Describe this scenario to pupils:

> Imagine a country called Monty. It is a democratic country. It has a prime minister and government elected by the people who vote in elections. It has its own declaration of rights, including freedom of speech. It has four national newspapers, six national television stations and one radio channel. Three of these newspapers, five of the television stations and the radio channel are owned by one person. That person is also the prime minister.

- What reactions do the pupils have to Monty?
- What problems might there be in Monty?
- How democratic is Monty?
- Does it have freedom of speech?
- How could the prime minister use the media to get and keep power?
- How could citizens of a country like Monty try to solve the problems?
- How far-fetched do the pupils think this story is?
- Can they find out which countries today have a similar situation to Monty?

Tell the pupils they all work for the prime minister as newspaper editors. They must edit the following piece, which has been written by a foreign journalist. It will be on the front page. It must be favourable to the prime minister or they will lose their job. The final article must be between 50 and 80 words.

> Last week I visited Monty, that small democratic republic lying in the middle of Europe. The people I spoke to complained bitterly about the problems they are having. 'Unemployment is rising, the price of food is rising', they muttered in low voices. I got the impression that some were frightened in case they were overheard! Yet Monty is a democracy with a long history of tolerance and freedom. This is the country where others have fled to as refugees from persecution. This is the country where trade grew because they allowed their citizens to think for themselves. This is the country where music and art flourished because they allowed their citizens to express themselves freely. This is the country where, in the past, government has listened to the people and everyone has benefited. A great country – but is it all changing now?

Discuss the fact that organisations and corporations can own information as well as individuals, as in the example of Monty.

What difference might it make in today's world to be:

- illiterate
- without ICT?

The organisations listed below have all taken action or are taking action for freedom of speech. Pupils choose one to research and make a short film (3 minutes) or write a short bulletin about their aims, methods and achievements. Tell pupils they must:

- Make the story a balanced one
- Make the story interesting and engaging.

> FAIR (Fairness and Accuracy in Reporting)
> Amnesty International
> Liberty
> Campaign for Press and Broadcasting Freedom
> Worldwatch Institute
> Press Wise Trust
> Independent Media Centre

Useful Contacts

General

Department for Education and Skills
Lists useful organisations.
www.dfes.gov.uk
Telephone 0845 602 2260

Citizenship Foundation
Has resources, ideas and publications.
www.citfou.org.uk
Telephone 020 7929 3344

Institute of Citizenship
Has a range of resources to support schools.
www.citizen.org.uk
Telephone 020 7929 5090

Council for Education in World Citizenship
Produces resources and supports partnerships world wide to promote citizenship.
www.csv.org.uk
Telephone 020 7278 6601

Newsround
Website has interesting information that is relevant for citizenship and aimed specifically at a young audience.
BBC.org.uk/newsround

Chapter 1
Refugee Council
www.refugeecouncil.org.uk
Telephone 020 7820 3000

Amnesty International
www.amnesty.org.uk
Telephone 020 7814 6200

Runnymede Trust
Organisation for racial equality, which produces excellent resources including the Homebeats and CD-ROM.
www.runnymedetrust.org.uk
Telephone 020 7377 9222

Commission for Racial Equality
Organisation for racial equality which produces useful information, reports and educational resources.
www.cre.gov.uk
Telephone 020 7828 7022

Equal Opportunities Commission
www.eoc.org.uk
Telephone 0845 601 5901

Home Office
Public information website:
www.statistics.gov.uk

Brit Kid
A website that explores identity and diversity for teenagers.
www.britkid.org.uk

Chapter 2
NSPCC (National Society for the Prevention of Cruelty to Children)
A support, pressure and information group for and about children.
www.nspcc.org.uk
Telephone 020 7825 2500

Children's Society
A support, pressure and information group for and about children.
www.the-childrens-society.org.uk
Telephone 020 7841 4436

Amnesty International
A charity campaigning for human rights. They produce resources on a range of human rights issues.
www.amnesty.org.uk
Telephone 020 7814 6200

Oxfam
An organisation for world peace and environmental safety.
www.oxfam.org.uk
Telephone 01865 312610

Liberty
An organisation for human rights.
www.liberty-human-rights.org.uk
Telephone 020 7403 3888

The Anti Slavery Organisation
www.antislavery.org.uk
Telephone 020 7501 8920

Equal Opportunities Commission
www.eoc.org.uk
Telephone 0845 601 5901

Chapter 3
Crown Prosecution Service
Website gives information on how the CPS handles different cases.
www.cps.gov.uk
Telephone 020 7796 8500

The Magistrates Association
Has a very useful website with resources for schools, links to other websites and useful advice on how to prepare and conduct a visit to a court as well as how to prepare for a visit to school by a local magistrate.
www.magistrates-association.org.uk
Telephone 020 7387 2353

UK Law Online
A useful resource for teachers wanting to know how the law works. The concepts and language are challenging for Key Stage 3 pupils.
www.leeds.ac.uk/law/hamlyn

YourTurn.Net
A very useful website for young people covering all kinds of topics in an accessible, clear and lively way. It has excellent information on the legal system and links to other useful sites.
www.yourturn.net

Chapter 4

Electoral Reform Society

A pressure group for voting reform. It has useful resources and online information about voting, including statistics of all General Election results and electoral turnout since 1945 and comparisons of voter turnout in European countries.
www.electoral-reform.org.uk
Telephone 020 7928 1622

European Union

Has information about and links to political parties across Europe.
www.2polis.net/enparties

The Register of Political Parties in the UK

Has list of all parties and links to all. Also basic information on each party.
www.party-register.gov.uk

Houses of Parliament

Lots of useful information and links to government departments.
www.parliament.uk

Charter 88

A pressure group for electoral reform that has a useful website.
www.charter 88.org.uk
Telephone 020 8880 6088
Also has online educational resources at *citizen21.org.uk*

'Make Women's Votes Count'

A campaign by the Fawcett Society. Packs available.
www.fawcett.gn.apc.org.uk

'Operation Black Vote'

A pressure group dedicated to getting more black people to vote. Website provides information and resources.
www.obv.org.uk
Telephone 020 8880 6061

Schools Council UK

Promotes political structures promoting youth involvement at school and beyond.
www.scocon.demon.co.uk
Telephone 020 8349 2459

Welsh Assembly

www.assembly.wales.gov.uk

Scottish Parliament
www.scottish.parliament.gov.uk

Northern Ireland Assembly
www.ni-assembly.gov.uk

Conservative Party
www.tory.org.uk

Labour Party
www.labour.org.uk

Liberal Democrat Party
www.libdems.org.uk

Green Party
www.greenparty.org.uk

Plaid Cymru – the Welsh National Party
www.plaidcymru.org.uk

Scottish National Party
www.snp.org.uk

Sinn Fein – Irish Republican Party
www.sinnfein.org.uk

Democratic Unionist Party (Northern Ireland)
www.dup.org.uk

Ulster Unionist Party
www.uup.org.uk

Chapter 5
Association for Science Education
Has excellent resources for science and citizenship, including a CD-ROM for schools called 'Can we; should we?' The CD-ROM can be viewed at *www.sycd.co.uk* and ordered via *jenifer.burden@scienceyear.com*
Telephone 01707 283001

Council for Environmental Education
Provides resources and a directory of useful organisations.
www.cee.org.uk
Telephone 0118 959 2550

Department of Trade and Industry and
Department for Environment, Farming, Rural Affairs
Both have websites with useful information on the environment, including policies, targets, statistics, graphs, summaries of enquiries.
www.dti.gov.uk
www.defra.gov.uk

Government website on sustainable development
www. sustainable-development.gov.uk

Centre for Alternative Technology, Machynlleth, Wales
A community that follows sustainable development principles. They provide courses and resources for teachers and pupils.
www.cat.org.uk
Telephone 01654 705950

Community Service Volunteers (CSV)
www.newnet.org.uk/csvnat.htm
Telephone 020 7278 6601

Go MAD (Make a Difference) 365 Daily Ways to Save the Planet
www.theecologist.org.uk

Friends of the Earth
An environmental pressure and information group.
www.foe.co.uk
Telephone 020 7490 1555

Greenpeace
An environmental pressure and information group.
www.greenpeace.org.uk
Telephone 020 7865 8100

National Society for Clean Air
Mstevens@nsca.org.uk

RSPB
Organisation for the protection of and information about birds, including educational resources.
www.rspb.org.uk
Telephone 01767 680551

World Wildlife Fund
www.wwf-uk.org.uk
Telephone 01483 412549

Climate Action Network
can-uk@wcl.org.uk
Telephone 020 7793 9296

The website *www.carboncalculator.org.uk* will measure the impact of energy use in your own home.

Energy saving tips can be found at *www.saveenergy.co.uk* and *www.globalaction-plan.org.uk*

Information about a wind-powered school can be found at *www.cassopschool.org.uk*

British Gas
Produces resources and runs competitions to do with saving energy in the home.
www.gas.co.uk

RSPCA
Charity working for welfare of animals. Has a range of information (none too distressing) on its website and runs campaigns for animal rights. Produces some resources, including free campaign pamphlets.
www.rspca.org.uk
Telephone 0870 3335 999

Department for Environment, Farming, Rural Affairs (Defra)
Has a website with the outcomes of the inquiry into fox hunting 2001.
www.huntinginquiry.gov.uk

Disability Rights Commission
www.drc-gb.org/drc/default.asp
Telephone 0845 762 2633

RNIB (Royal National Institute for the Blind)
Support and information group.
www.rnib.org.uk
Telephone 0845 766 9999

RNID (Royal National Institute for the Deaf)
Support and information group.
www.rnid.org.uk
Telephone 08088 080123

Radar
Disability network.
www.radar.org.uk
Telephone 020 7250 3222

Chapter 6
The following are all committed to improving freedom of speech

FAIR (Fairness and Accuracy in Reporting)
www.fair.org.uk

Amnesty International (as above)

Liberty (as above)

Campaign for Press and Broadcasting Freedom
http://keywordas.dsvr.co.uk/freepress

Worldwatch Institute
www.worldwatch.org.uk

Press Wise Trust
www.presswise.org.uk

Independent Media Centre
www.Indymedia.org.uk

There is an online newspaper for 8 to 18 year olds at *express.org.uk*. It contains articles and reports on youth issues written by young people.

Useful information and resources can be found at *www.mediaEd.org.uk*.

Appendix A: Assessment for learning: Making progress in citizenship

In assessing achievements and progression in citizenship, teachers will need to think about progression in areas they may not have considered before. For example, what does getting better in listening look like? How can we assess the values of pupils?

The questions below are intended to help teachers make assessments in the key areas of citizenship.

Reflection

In reflecting on progress in citizenship, pupils will need to reflect on their personal beliefs, attitudes and how these might have changed and why.

Reflection on pupil as learner

What did I find difficult?
What helped me to move on (e.g. group work, teacher, textbook, discussion, etc.)?
What am I finding difficult now?
What could I use to help me move on?

What did I find out during that activity (role play, survey, conversation, etc.)?
How did it make me feel? Why?
What new ideas and thoughts did it give me? How?
What would I like to think/know now?

Reflection on beliefs, values, attitudes

What my ideas were at the start/What I thought about ______________________ at the start.
How my ideas have changed and why.
What I contributed to . . . . . .
What else I would like to know/discuss.

Where did my ideas come from? Home? Media? Friends? School?
What didn't I know or understand before . . . . . .
What I do know or understand after . . . . . .

At first I believed/thought this ________________________ was important/most important.
Then I thought this . . . . . .
I changed my mind because of . . . . . .

Why have my ideas, beliefs, attitudes, values changed between ________________________ and ________________________? For example, because of:

- More knowledge
- Different knowledge
- Talking and listening to others
- Change in my personal life
- Getting older
- Situation/issue has changed
- Different circumstances/experiences

I cannot make up my mind.
I can see this 'side' because I agree that ________________________
And I can see the other side because I also agree that ________________________

Progression in discussion and communication

Below are different stages of progression in discussion and communication skills.

Stage 1
I listened to others.
I said what I thought/believed.
I spoke clearly.
I took part in the group.
I used my knowledge and understanding – what I knew – in the discussion.

Stage 2
I gave suggestions and ideas to help the group.
I showed I was listening by looking at the speaker and using body language.
I showed I was listening by remembering accurately what other people said.
I reacted to what others said by agreeing or disagreeing.
I used my knowledge and understanding – what I knew – to make points.
I helped others take turns to speak.

Stage 3
I backed up my opinions with reasons, facts, explanations.
I showed I was listening by taking on board other points of view.
I showed I was listening by my facial expressions and body language.
I encouraged others to speak by looking at them, inviting them to speak, etc.
I made positive encouraging comments to help others take part.
I moved the discussion forward by . . . . . .
I recognised different and conflicting views.
I accurately represented the views of others.

Appendix B: Assessment: Using a range of assessors

Self assessment

Self assessment is a vital part of citizenship education. This is partly because citizenship is about reflection and because self assessment enables pupils to understand and manage their own progress in areas such as participation, knowledge and understanding, communication. It also enables them to recognise their own beliefs, ideas, attitudes and to reflect on changes in their beliefs. However, teachers will need to take care with self assessment that particular groups of pupils do not underestimate their progress and others do not overestimate their progress. Peer and teacher assessment can be used effectively to moderate self assessments.

The sentence stems below are helpful to pupils doing self assessments. Remember to make clear the assessment criteria by which the pupils are to judge their performance.

My best achievement was . . . . . .
I solved problems with learning by . . . . . .
I found these people could help . . . . . .
I found these tactics could help . . . . . .
At the start I thought/knew this . . . . . .
By the end I thought/knew this . . . . . .
I changed my mind about . . . . . .
I changed my mind because . . . . . .

In the area of 'participation' (taking part) I achieved this . . . . . .
In the area of 'communication' (speaking and listening) I achieved this . . . . . .
In the area of 'organisation' (making something happen) I achieved this . . . . . .
In the area of 'presentation' (doing something for an audience) I achieved this . . . . . .

Design a Self Assessment Sheet that can be used for a wide range of self-assessments about different activities. The following is an example of a generic Self Assessment Sheet.

Assessment criteria	Always	Often	Sometimes	Rarely
Listened to others				

Peer assessment

Peer assessment can be used to assess group participation and responsibility as well as being used to assess the performance of other individuals in the classroom.

Before doing any peer assessment, agree ground rules first. For example, any feedback to peers must be:

- positive
- useful
- relevant to the Learning Objectives/Assessment Criteria

Structure for peer assessment
Design a Peer Assessment Sheet that can be used for a wide range of peer assessments about different activities. The following is an example of a generic Peer Assessment Sheet.

Assessment criteria	Always	Often	Sometimes	Rarely
Listened to others				

At the end of an activity, each pupil can *either*:

- Fill in a sheet about themselves
- Circulate sheets

Do peers agree/disagree with self assessments?
Pupils have chance to change self assessments

or

- Fill in a sheet about a peer
- Circulate sheets

Do pupils agree/disagree with peer assessments?
Peers have chance to change their assessments of others

Peer assessment of group work
Did we all participate?
Did we support each other?
Were roles and responsibilities shared out fairly?
Did we stay on task?
Did we achieve what we meant to achieve?

Community partner assessment

When working with community partners (mentors, visitors, guides, speakers, etc.) make sure that:

(i) You both agree and understand the Learning Objectives.
(ii) Interview questions for assessment feedback are designed by both of you or fully understood by both of you.
(iii) In designing questions, make sure they:
- Focus on the objectives
- Lead to important and relevant information about achievement
- Lead to answers which are useful for pupils and help them make progress
- Arise out of the particular expertise of your community partner

Appendix C: Ground rules for discussion and debate

You may wish to negotiate ground rules with pupils. The following could be used, therefore, as a stimulus or could be displayed in the classroom as 'rules'.

Take responsibility

- Start statements with 'I believe ......' or 'It is my own opinion ......', rather than 'You're wrong ......'.
- Say what you believe or think, share your opinions, thoughts and beliefs with others.

Respect others

- Listen to what others are saying.
- Never use abusive language.
- Respect differences of belief and opinion.

Back up your beliefs

- Give reasons or evidence to back up your beliefs. For example 'I believe this ...... because I know/think that ......'.

Be real/honest

- If you are unsure, then say so. For example, 'I'm not sure what I believe ......' or 'I think it's possible that ......'.
- Take responsibility for your beliefs. Say what you think *during* the discussion.